Everyman's Poetry

Everyman, I will go with thee,
and be thy guide

George Crabbe

Selected and edited by STEPHEN DERRY

University of Bristol

EVERYMAN
J. M. Dent · London

This edition first published by Everyman Paperbacks in 1999
Selection, introduction and other critical apparatus
© J. M. Dent 1999

J. M. Dent
Orion Publishing Group
Orion House
5 Upper St Martin's Lane
London WC2H 9EA

Typeset by Deltatype Ltd, Birkenhead, Merseyside
Printed in Great Britain by
The Guernsey Press Co. Ltd, Guernsey, C.I.

British Library Cataloguing-in-Publication
Data is available on request

ISBN 0 460 88205 8

Contents

Note on the Author and Editor

GEORGE CRABBE (1754–1832) was born in Aldborough (now Aldeburgh), Suffolk, the son of a collector of salt duties. He served an apprenticeship as an apothecary, and practised briefly and unsuccessfully; he also worked as a labourer. In 1775 he published his poem *Inebriety* anonymously in Ipswich, and in 1780 he moved to London, intent on a literary career. He expressed his ambitions in *The Candidate* (1780). Nearly destitute, he acquired the patronage of Edmund Burke, through whom he met such figures as Charles James Fox and Joshua Reynolds. Burke's patronage enabled him to enter the Church, and in 1782 he became domestic chaplain to the Duke of Rutland. In 1783 he married Sarah Elmy, whom he had known since 1772, and published *The Village*, after it had been lightly revised by Dr Johnson. After *The Newspaper* (1785), Crabbe published no more poetry until 1807, though he produced several works on natural history, and wrote three novels, which he subsequently destroyed. From 1784 until 1814 he held clerical offices in Leicestershire, but for most of this period he was an absentee clergyman, living in rural Suffolk. From 1794 until her death in 1813 his wife suffered a depressive illness, which cast a shadow over Crabbe's life. In 1807 his new poem *The Parish Register* appeared, followed by *The Borough* (1810) and *Tales* (1812). In 1814 Crabbe moved to Trowbridge, Wiltshire, where he spent the rest of his life. Crabbe only once left England, to visit his friend Walter Scott in Edinburgh in 1822. *Tales of the Hall* (1819) was the last important work published in his lifetime, whilst the major poems of his final years appeared as *Posthumous Tales* in the eight-volume edition of his *Poetical Works* (1834).

STEPHEN DERRY is a teacher in Continuing Education at Bristol University. He has contributed to such journals as *English Language Notes*, *Foundation*, *Notes and Queries*, *Persuasions*, *The Thomas Hardy Journal*, and *Trivium*.

Chronology of Crabbe's Life

Year	Age	Life
1754		(24 December) Born at Aldeburgh (then called Aldborough), Suffolk, to George Crabbe and his wife Mary (née Lodwick)
1762	8	Starts at a school in Bungay, Suffolk (until 1766)
1766	12	Starts at a school in Stowmarket, Suffolk (until 1768)
1768	14	Apprenticed to an apothecary at Wickhambrook, Suffolk
1771	17	Apprenticed to an apothecary at Woodbridge, Suffolk
1772	18	Meets his future wife Sarah Elmy. First poems published in the *Lady's Magazine*

Chronology of his Times

Year	Literary Context	Historical Context
1754	Death of Fielding	Duke of Newcastle Prime Minister
1755	Johnson, *Dictionary of the English Language*	
1756	Birth of Godwin	Black Hole of Calcutta. Start of Seven Years War
1757	Birth of Blake	
1758		Birth of Nelson
1759	Johnson, *Rasselas* Birth of Burns	
1760		Death of George II. Accession of George III
1762	Goldsmith, *The Citizen of the World*	
1763	Death of Shenstone	
1764	Walpole, *The Castle of Otranto*	
1766	Goldsmith, *The Vicar of Wakefield*	Death of the Old Pretender
1768	Sterne, *A Sentimental Journey*	Founding of the Royal Academy
1769	First 'Junius' letters in *Public Advertiser*	Births of Napoleon, Wellington
1770	Goldsmith, *The Deserted Village* Birth of Wordworth	
1771	Birth of Scott Deaths of Gray, Smollett	
1772	Graves, *The Spiritual Quixote* Birth of Coleridge	

Year	Age	Life
1775	21	Employed as a labourer, then as an apothecary and surgeon, in and around Aldeburgh. *Inebriety* published anonymously in Ipswich
1780	26	Moves to London. Witnesses the Gordon Riots. *The Candidate* published
1781	27	Burke becomes his patron. Meets Fox and Reynolds. Ordained deacon. *The Library* published
1782	28	Back in Aldeburgh as a curate, he is unhappy with his reception. Ordained priest. Becomes domestic chaplain to Duke of Rutland at Belvoir
1783	29	Marries Sarah Elmy. *The Village* published
1784	30	Becomes a curate in Leicestershire
1785	31	Birth of son, George. *The Newspaper* published
1786	32	Death of his father
1789	35	Awarded Lambeth LL.B. degree
1790	36	Starts taking opium, on medical advice
1791	37	Moves to Suffolk, though retaining his living in Leicestershire
1794	40	Sarah starts to suffer from a depressive illness

Year	Literary Context	Historical Context
1773	Birth of Jeffrey	Boston Tea Party
1774	Birth of Southey	Priestley discovers oxygen
	Death of Goldsmith	
1775	Birth of Austen	
1776		American Declaration of Independence
1778	Burney, *Evelina*	
1780		First running of the Derby
1782	Burney, *Cecilia*	
1783	Blake, *Poetical Sketches*	
1784	Death of Johnson	John Wesley ordains a minister, in an act of schism
1785	Cowper, *The Task*	
1786	Beckford, *Vathek*	
1788	Birth of Byron	Death of Charles Wesley
1789	White, *Natural History . . . of Selborne*	Start of French Revolution
1790	Burke, *Reflections on the Revolution in France*	
1791	Paine, *Rights of Man*	Death of John Wesley
	Birth of Shelley	
1792	Death of Reynolds	
1793	Godwin, *Enquiry Concerning Political Justice*	Britain and France at war
1794	Godwin, *Caleb Williams*	
1795	Birth of Keats	
1796	Inchbald, *Nature and Art*	
	Death of Burns	
1797	Death of Burke	Naval mutinies at Spithead and the Nore

Year	*Age*	*Life*
1801–2	47	Writes and destroys three novels
1806	52	Returns to Leicestershire, to find Methodism has flourished in his absence
1807	53	*Poems* published, included *The Parish Register*
1810	56	*The Borough* published
1812	58	*Tales* published
1813	59	Death of his wife
1814	60	Moves to Trowbridge, Wiltshire
1816	62	Experiences riots in Trowbridge

Year	Literary Context	Historical Context
1798	Wordsworth and Coleridge, *Lyrical Ballads*	
1800	Edgeworth, *Castle Rackrent* Death of Cowper	
1801		Birth of Newman
1802	*Edinburgh Review* first published	Peace of Amiens
1804		Napoleon crowned Emperor
1805	Scott, *The Lay of the Last Minstrel*	Battle of Trafalgar
1806		Deaths of Fox, Pitt
1807	Byron, *Hours of Idleness*	Abolition of the slave trade
1808	Scott, *Marmion*	Start of Peninsular War
1809	Births of Tennyson, Edward Fitzgerald	
1810	Southey, *The Curse of Kehama*	Prince of Wales becomes Prince Regent
1811	Austen, *Sense and Sensibility*	
1812	Births of Dickens, Browning	Assassination of Prime Minister Spencer Perceval
1813	Austen, *Pride and Prejudice*	
1814	Austen, *Mansfield Park* Scott, *Waverley*	Napoleon exiled to Elba
1815		Battle of Waterloo
1816	Austen, *Emma* Coleridge, *Christabel*	Elgin Marbles placed in British Museum
1817	Death of Austen Scott, *Rob Roy*	
1818	Keats, *Endymion* Mary Shelley, *Frankenstein*	Birth of Marx

Year	Literary Context	Historical Context
1819	Shelley, *Masque of Anarchy* Births of Whitman, George Eliot	Peterloo Massacre
1820	Keats, *Lamia . . . and Other Poems*	Death of George III. Accession of George IV
1821	Shelley, *Adonais* Death of Keats	Death of Napoleon
1822	Birth of Arnold. Death of Shelley	
1824	Death of Byron	
1825		Stockton–Darlington railway
1827	Death of Blake	
1829		Catholic Emancipation Act
1830	Tennyson, *Poems, Chiefly Lyrical*	Death of George IV. Accession of William IV.
1832	Death of Scott	Great Reform Act
1834	Death of Coleridge	Tolpuddle Martyrs

Introduction

When Robert Southey sought for a word to describe George Crabbe as a poet, he found that he had to make one up: antithesizer. In a letter of September 1808 he wrote that Crabbe 'is an imitator, or rather an *antithesizer*, of Goldsmith.'[1] This is the only occurrence of the word in the *OED*, where it is defined, not altogether helpfully, as 'one who antithesizes or forms an antithesis'. The specific point that Southey is making is that in *The Village* – the most famous of his poems at that time – Crabbe opposed the celebration of pastoral life found in Goldsmith's poem *The Deserted Village* (1770) with a picture drawn from his first-hand experience of growing up amidst the harsh realities of the poverty-stricken rural Suffolk coast. *The Deserted Village* was one of the most popular of many examples of pastoral poetry which Crabbe felt gave a false impression of rural life, evading or ignoring the hardship of the human struggle with Nature, and the damaging effects of poverty on everyday existence. Crabbe made his opposition to this kind of poetry explicit: 'I paint the Cot,/ As Truth will paint it, and as Bards will not.'

Crabbe was an antithesizer of more authors than Goldsmith, and he had taken up this role virtually from the start of his poetic career. His first important poem, *Inebriety*, published when he was twenty-one, is an oppositional response to John Gay's poem, 'Wine' (1708). Like *Inebriety*, 'Wine' is an early work, and also like *Inebriety*, is an exercise in stylistic imitation of an earlier poet: Milton in Gay's case, Pope in Crabbe's. Whilst Crabbe imitates Pope's style and language, the content of *Inebriety* concerns those aspects of alcoholic consumption which Gay ignored: the darker aspects, drunkenness and its associated vices.

Crabbe actually seems to have needed a model to argue against to produce his best in poetry in the eighteenth-century phase of his career: *The Newspaper* illustrates this. Crabbe's main claim for the poem is its novelty of subject, but this is also its liability: with no falsifying predecessor to correct, Crabbe's poem becomes, after a lively start, rather aimless and rather dull. It also carries imitation of Pope to and maybe beyond the boundaries of parody, as one of its first critics, Charles Burney, complained.[2]

But Crabbe was not just an anthithesizer of eighteenth-century poetic models. In April 1808, a few months before Southey wrote his letter, a review of Crabbe's *Poems* had appeared in the influential and prestigious *Edinburgh Review*, written by the editor, Francis Jeffrey. This paid most attention to Crabbe's old and new rural poems, *The Village* and *The Parish Register*, and used them as a stick with which to berate a group of writers Jeffrey strongly disliked: the Lake Poets. Jeffrey set Crabbe up as a model of good sense and good practice; essentially, he saw Crabbe as an antithesizer of Southey and his associates:

> There is one set of writers, indeed, from whose works those of Mr Crabbe might receive all that elucidation which results from contrast, and from an entire opposition in all points of taste and opinion. We allude now to the Wordsworths, and the Southeys, and Coleridges, and all that misguided frater-nity . . . These gentlemen write a good deal about rustic life, as well as Mr Crabbe; and they even agree with him on dwelling much on its discomforts; but nothing can be more opposite than the views they take of the subject, or the manner in which they execute their representation of them.[3]

(That poets dealing with such subjects presented a more balanced picture may have been due in part to Crabbe: selections from *The Village* were reprinted in the popular *Elegant Extracts*, and Words-worth for one recorded that they made a considerable impression upon his youthful feelings.) For Jeffrey, Crabbe's down-to-earth, detailed poetry, eschewing philosophical fancies or metaphysical speculations, 'exhibits the common people of England pretty much as they are, and as they must appear to every one who will take the trouble of examining into their condition'. Crabbe 'shows us something which we have all seen, or may see, in real life; and draws from it such feelings and such reflections as every human being must acknowledge that it is calculated to excite'. By contrast, 'the gentlemen of the new school' virtually ignore 'any description of persons that are at all known to the common inhabitants of the world'. Rather they

> invent for themselves certain whimsical and unheard of beings, to whom they impute some fantastical combination of

feelings, and labour to excite our sympathy for them, either
by placing them in incredible situations, or by some strained
and exaggerated moralization of a vague and tragical
description.

However heretical later generations may have found these
remarks, the reading public of the day agreed with Jeffrey, for
Crabbe became a popular favourite and his poems bestsellers.

In his Preface to the *Tales* (1812), which is the nearest Crabbe
ever came to producing a poetic manifesto, he seems to have had
Jeffrey's 1808 review in mind, for in it he criticizes the Romantic
idea of a poet, which he felt was too narrowly and exclusively
defined. The notion that a poet was somehow set apart from other
men, with finer intuitions and special powers, was anathema to
Crabbe. He did not name names – Crabbe disliked making personal
criticism, as his short poem 'Satire' makes clear – but his targets are
obvious. A Romantic poet, in Crabbe's view, 'lights upon a kind of
fairyland, in which he places a creation of his own'; he captures his
readers' imaginations and 'elevates them above the grossness of
actual being'; the figures in this fairyland are not real people but
'visionary inhabitants'[4] (both seen in a vision and seers of visions).
Such things are very fine: but they would deny Crabbe, whose
talent is that of 'describing, as faithfully as I could, men, manners,
and things' – in other words, describing 'actual being' – the title of
poet. And they would also in Crabbe's eyes remove that title from
Chaucer, and Dryden, and Pope (who would be reduced to the
status of a mere 'elegant versifier').

It seems likely that before Jeffrey's review, Crabbe had been an
inadvertent antithesizer of Romantic poetry, which he does not
seem to have known well. Jeffrey's advocacy forced him to identify
himself as a conscious antithesizer. His most sympathetic critic had,
it appears, coaxed from him his most articulate and polemical
statement about poetry.

Crabbe has so far been considered in terms of who and what
he was not, but there are authors whom he resembles, with whom
he does not have an oppositional relationship. In his Preface he
implicitly placed himself in a tradition starting with Chaucer,
which produces 'satire wherein character is skilfully delineated'.
Chaucer's narratives contain 'many pages of coarse, accurate, and
minute, but very striking description'. By implication, this legiti-
mizes the 'lowness' of Crabbe's highly-detailed writing, of which

critics had complained. Dryden, and of course Pope, were other predecessors with whom he allied himself, as his defence of them demonstrated.

Crabbe's nineteenth-century critics, however, when searching for comparisons, often stepped outside literature entirely, and invoked the visual arts. In 1808 the *Annual Review* commented 'Crabbe is a kind of Dutch painter, who draws nothing that he does not, and anything that he does see'.[5] Dutch painting was not then highly regarded, so this was not much of a compliment, especially as it hinted at a want of selectivity (an accusation others made overtly): but the comparison was to be frequently repeated. An only slightly less popular comparison was with Hogarth: this seems to have begun with Thomas Denman in 1810, who regarded as similar the 'force and truth' of their descriptions, 'the moral effect of their combinations', and 'their insight into human nature'.[6] As Crabbe became more interested in and confident about narrative poetry, until this became the form most associated with him, so the parallels with Hogarth's sequences increased, with their moral commentaries in both cases embedded in rich detail.

Other critics have seen Crabbe in terms of novelists: he has been regarded as a successor both to Richardson (on the grounds of social documentation and investigation of the human psyche) and Fielding (on the grounds of vigour, hatred of falsehood, and 'lowness'). He has also been seen as a precursor of Dickens and George Eliot (who read Crabbe in her teens with enjoyment). But the novelist with whom Crabbe has the greatest affinity is Jane Austen. Both share a background of rural Anglicanism; both were denied prestigious education for reasons of class or gender. Both are notable for realistic social detail, psychological insight, and revelations of character through speech. Both are moral writers, rarely overtly didactic, and essentially conservative satirists. Austen's irony has its equivalent in Crabbe's sly sardonicism. The similarity increases in the *Tales* and its successors, in which Crabbe's milieu shifts towards the middle class, amongst whom there are perhaps more storytelling opportunities. Austen admired Crabbe to the extent of playfully fantasizing about marrying him. She also named the heroine of her novel *Mansfield Park*, Fanny Price, after a character in *The Parish Register*: both are virtuous young women who attract the unwanted attentions of a wealthy rake. To point up the link with Crabbe, Austen makes her Fanny Price a possessor of the *Tales*.

From 1790 Crabbe took opium for medicinal purposes, but he kept his habit under control, and it seems to have had little impact on his writing, in contrast to Romantic opium-takers like Coleridge. But he did share an interest with Coleridge in miscellaneous scientific information, and published on natural history. Botany and geology especially interested Crabbe. The botanical content of Crabbe's poems resembles that found in the later works of one of the most popular novelists of the 1790s, Charlotte Smith, making her perhaps his closest equivalent in this respect amongst his contemporaries. Her prose descriptions of bleak landscapes also link her with Crabbe, whom George Gilfillan characterized as 'the Poet of the waste places of Creation'.[7]

The Victorian canon-formers largely ignored Crabbe. His social realism was for them the province of the novel, whilst his poetry lacked those favoured Victorian qualities of uplift, lyricism, and vaguely mysterious visionary implications. In the twentieth century, the supposed desirability of difficulty in poetry has led to Crabbe being overlooked, it being supposed that his work is simple and straightforward (which it is not, any more than life itself is). Crabbe was a disappointment for those looking for political engagement, especially for those expecting a poet of the poor to speak up for them in radical terms. Although *The Village* identifies a problem, and is in parts Crabbe's most passionately felt poem, it does not offer any kind of political solution. Nearly forty years later, Crabbe produced *Smugglers and Poachers*, of which the same can be said: he illustrates the ferocity of the Game Laws, and indicates the complicity of many sections of society in breaking them, but puts forward no distinctly political solution. A Victorian critic said Crabbe's view of the world was not poetical because for him it was 'a place full of stupid mistakes, bungles, and errors'.[8] It is also not political: for Crabbe, politics were a component and a cause of mistakes and bungles, not a cure for them. Crabbe did have admirers, including Fitzgerald, T. S. Eliot, Forster, and Leavis, but they all took a rather pessimistic line about the chances of reviving his popularity. Today, the cultural visibility of Crabbe's prolific output has been reduced to one poem, *Peter Grimes*, which is itself best known through the mediation of Benjamin Britten's opera. But the opera's Grimes is very different from the poem's: Crabbe's sordid

murderer is transformed by Britten and his librettist Montagu
Slater into a man more sinned against than sinning, a victim of
society, a misunderstood Romantic hero – one of Jeffrey's 'whimsi-
cal and unheard of beings'. Ironically, Crabbe himself has been
antithesized.

STEPHEN DERRY

References

1. Cited from *Crabbe: The Critical Heritage*, ed. Arthur Pollard (London and
   Boston: Routledge and Kegan Paul, 1972), p. 293.
2. See *Crabbe: The Critical Heritage*. p. 46.
3. Jeffrey's review is cited from *Crabbe: The Critical Heritage*, pp. 56–7.
4. Cited from *George Crabbe: Poems*, ed. A. W. Ward, 3 vols (Cambridge:
   CUP, 1905–07), ii, pp. 8–11.
5. Cited from *Crabbe: The Critical Heritage*, p. 64.
6. Cited from *Crabbe: The Critical Heritage*, p. 80.
7. Cited from *Crabbe: The Critical Heritage*, p. 376.
8. Cited from *Crabbe: The Critical Heritage*, p. 416.

George Crabbe

Inebriety

Part the First

The mighty Spirit and its power which stains
The bloodless cheek, and vivifies the brains,
I sing. Say ye, its fiery Vot'ries true,
The jovial Curate, and the shrill-tongu'd Shrew;
Ye, in the floods of limpid poison nurst,   5
Where Bowl the second charms like Bowl the first;
Say, how and why the sparkling ill is shed,
The Heart which hardens, and which rules the Head.
When Winter stern his gloomy front uprears,
A sable void the barren earth appears;   10
The meads no more their former verdure boast,
Fast bound their streams, and all their Beauty lost;
The herds, the flocks, their icy garments mourn,
And wildly murmur for the Spring's return;
The fallen branches from the sapless tree   15
With glittering fragments strow the glassy way;
From snow-top'd Hills the whirlwinds keenly blow,
Howl through the Woods, and pierce the vales below;
Through the sharp air a flaky torrent flies,
Mocks the slow sight, and hides the gloomy skies;   20
The fleecy clouds their chilly bosoms bare,
And shed their substance on the floating air;
The floating air their downy substance glides
Through springing Waters, and prevents their tides;
Seizes the rolling Waves, and, as a God,   25
Charms their swift race, and stops the refl'ent flood;
The opening valves, which fill the venal road,
Then scarcely urge along the sanguine flood;
The labouring Pulse a slower motion rules,
The Tendons stiffen, and the Spirit cools;   30
Each asks the aid of Nature's sister Art,
To chear the senses, and to warm the Heart.

The gentle fair on nervous tea relies,
Whilst gay good-nature sparkles in her eyes;
An inoffensive Scandal fluttering round,   35
Too rough to tickle, and too light to wound;
Champain the Courtier drinks, the spleen to chase,
The Colonel burgundy, and port his Grace;
Turtle and 'rrack the city rulers charm,
Ale and content the labouring peasants warm;   40
O'er the dull embers happy Colin sits,
Colin, the prince of joke and rural wits;
Whilst the wind whistles through the hollow panes,
He drinks, nor of the rude assault complains;
And tells the Tale, from sire to son retold,   45
Of spirits vanishing near hidden gold;
Of moon-clad Imps, that tremble by the dew,
Who skim the air, or glide o'er waters blue.
The throng invisible, that doubtless float
By mould'ring Tombs, and o'er the stagnant moat;   50
Fays dimly glancing on the russet plain,
And all the dreadful nothing of the Green.
And why not these? Less fictious is the tale,
Inspir'd by Hel'con's streams, than muddy ale?
Peace be to such, the happiest and the best,   55
Who with the forms of fancy urge their jest;
Who wage no war with an Avenger's Rod,
Nor in the pride of reason curse their God.
  When in the vaulted arch Lucina gleams,
And gaily dances o'er the azure streams;   60
When in the wide cerulean space on high
The vivid stars shoot lustre through the sky;
On silent Ether when a trembling sound
Reverberates, and wildly floats around,
Breaking through trackless space upon the ear –   65
Conclude the Bachanalian Rustic near;
O'er Hills and vales the jovial Savage reels,
Fire in his head and Frenzy at his heels;
From paths direct the bending Hero swerves,
And shapes his way in ill-proportion'd curves;   70
Now safe arriv'd, his sleeping Rib he calls,
And madly thunders on the muddy walls;

The well-known sounds an equal fury move,
For rage meets rage, as love enkindles love;
The buxom Quean from bed of flocks descends   75
With vengeful ire, a civil war portends,
An oaken plant the Hero's breast defends.
In vain the 'waken'd infant's accents shrill
The humble regions of the cottage fill;
In vain the Cricket chirps the mansion through,   80
'Tis war, and Blood and Battle must ensue.
As when, on humble stage, him Satan hight
Defies the brazen Hero to the fight;
From twanging strokes what dire misfortunes rise,
What fate to maple arms, and glassen eyes;   85
Here lies a leg of elm, and there a stroke
From ashen neck has whirl'd a Head of oak.
So drops from either power, with vengeance big,
A remnant night-cap, and an old cut wig;
Titles unmusical, retorted round,   90
On either ear with leaden vengeance sound;
'Till equal Valour equal Wounds create,
And drowsy peace concludes the fell debate;
Sleep in her woolen mantle wraps the pair,
And sheds her poppies on the ambient air;   95
Intoxication flies, as fury fled,
On rocky pinions quits the aching head;
Returning Reason cools the fiery blood,
And drives from memory's seat the rosy God.
Yet still he holds o'er some his madd'ning rule,   100
Still sways his Sceptre, and still knows his Fool;
Witness the livid lip and fiery front,
With many a smarting trophy plac'd upon't;
The hollow Eye, which plays in misty springs,
And the hoarse Voice, which rough and broken rings. 105
These are his triumphs, and o'er these he reigns,
The blinking Deity of reeling brains.
   See Inebriety! her wand she waves,
And lo! her pale, and lo! her purple slaves;
Sots in embroidery, and sots in crape,   110
Of every order, station, rank, and shape;
The King, who nods upon his rattle-throne;

The staggering Peer, to midnight revel prone;
The slow-tongu'd Bishop, and the Deacon sly,
The humble Pensioner, and Gownsman dry;   115
The proud, the mean, the selfish, and the great,
Swell the dull throng, and stagger into state.
    Lo! proud Flaminius at the splendid board,
The easy chaplain of an atheist Lord,
Quaffs the bright juice, with all the gust of sense,   120
And clouds his brain in torpid elegance;
In china vases see the sparkling ill,
From gay Decanters view the rosy rill;
The neat-carv'd pipes in silver settle laid,
The screw by mathematic cunning made;   125
The whole a pompous and enticing scene,
And grandly glaring for the surplic'd Swain;
Oh! happy Priest whose God like Egypt's lies,
At once the Deity and sacrifice!
But is Flaminius, then, the man alone,   130
To whom the Joys of swimming brains are known?
Lo! the poor Toper whose untutor'd sense
Sees bliss in ale, and can with wine dispense;
Whose head proud fancy never taught to steer
Beyond the muddy extacies of Beer;   135
But simple nature can her longing quench
Behind the settle's curve, or humbler bench;
Some kitchen-fire diffusing warmth around,
The semi-globe by Hieroglyphics crown'd;
Where canvas purse displays the brass enroll'd,   140
Nor Waiters rave, nor Landlords thirst for gold;
Ale and content his fancy's bounds confine,
He asks no limpid Punch, no rosy Wine;
But sees, admitted to an equal share,
Each faithful swain the heady potion bear.   145
Go, wiser thou! and in thy scale of taste
Weight gout and gravel against ale and rest.
Call vulgar palates, what thou judgest so;
Say, beer is heavy, windy, cold and slow;
Laugh at poor sots with insolent pretence,   150
Yet cry when tortur'd, where is Providence?
If thou alone art, head and heel, not clear,

Alone made steady here, untumour'd there;
Snatch from the Board the bottle and the bowl,
Curse the keen pain, and be a mad proud Fool.   155

Ye Gentle Gales

Ye gentle Gales, that softly move,
Go whisper to the Fair I love;
Tell her I languish and adore,
And pity in return implore.

But if she's cold to my request,   5
Ye louder Winds, proclaim the rest –
My sighs, my tears, my griefs proclaim,
And speak in strongest notes my flame.

Still if she rests in mute disdain,
And thinks I feel a common pain –   10
Wing'd with my woes, ye Tempests, fly,
And tell the haughty Fair I die.

The Comparison

Friendship is like the gold refined,
    And all may weigh its worth;
Love like the ore, brought undesign'd
    In virgin beauty forth.

Friendship may pass from age to age,   5
    And yet remain the same;
Love must in many a toil engage,
    And melt in lambent flame.

The Village

from **Book One**

I grant indeed that fields and flocks have charms
For him that grazes or for him that farms;
But when amid such pleasing scenes I trace
The poor laborious natives of the place,
And see the mid-day sun, with fervid ray,   5
On their bare heads and dewy temples play;
While some, with feebler heads and fainter hearts,
Deplore their fortune, yet sustain their parts –
Then shall I dare these real ills to hide
In tinsel trappings of poetic pride?   10
    No; cast by Fortune on a frowning coast,
Which neither groves nor happy valleys boast;
Where other cares than those the Muse relates,
And other shepherds dwell with other mates;
By such examples taught, I paint the Cot,   15
As Truth will paint it, and as Bards will not:
Nor you, ye Poor, of letter'd scorn complain,
To you the smoothest song is smooth in vain;
O'ercome by labour, and bow'd down by time,
Feel you the barren flattery of a rhyme?   20
Can poets soothe you, when you pine for bread,
By winding myrtles round your ruin'd shed?
Can their light tales your weighty griefs o'erpower,
Or glad with airy mirth the toilsome hour?
    Lo! where the heath, with withering brake grown o'er,   25
Lends the light turf that warms the neighbouring poor;
From thence a length of burning sand appears,
Where the thin harvest waves its wither'd ears;
Rank weeds, that every art and care defy,
Reign o'er the land, and rob the blighted rye: 30
There thistles stretch their prickly arms afar,
And to the ragged infant threaten war;

There poppies nodding, mock the hope of toil:
There the blue bugloss paints the sterile soil;
Hardy and high, above the slender sheaf, 35
The slimy mallow waves her silky leaf;
O'er the young shoot the charlock throws a shade,
And clasping tares cling round the sickly blade;
With mingled tints the rocky coasts abound,
And a sad splendour vainly shines around. 40
So looks the nymph whom wretched arts adorn,
Betray'd by man, then left for man to scorn;
Whose cheek in vain assumes the mimic rose,
While her sad eyes the troubled breast disclose;
Whose outward splendour is but folly's dress, 45
Exposing most, when most it gilds distress.
   Here joyless roam a wild amphibious race,
With sullen woe display'd in every face;
Who, far from civil arts and social fly,
And scowl at strangers with suspicious eye. 50
   Here too the lawless merchant of the main
Draws from his plough th' intoxicated swain;
Want only claim'd the labour of the day,
But vice now steals his nightly rest away.
   Where are the swains, who, daily labour done, 55
With rural games play'd down the setting sun;
Who struck with matchless force the bounding ball,
Or made the pond'rous quoit obliquely fall;
While some huge Ajax, terrible and strong,
Engaged some artful stripling of the throng, 60
And fell beneath him, foil'd, while far around
Hoarse triumph rose, and rocks return'd the sound?
Where now are these? – Beneath yon cliff they stand,
To show the freighted pinnace where to land;
To load the ready steed with guilty haste, 65
To fly in terror o'er the pathless waste,
Or, when detected, in their straggling course,
To foil their foes by cunning or by force;
Or, yielding part (which equal knaves demand),
To gain a lawless passport through the land. 70
   Here, wand'ring long, amid these frowning fields,
I sought the simple life that Nature yields;

Rapine and Wrong and Fear usurp'd her place,
And a bold, artful, surly, savage race;
Who, only skill'd to take the finny tribe,   75
The yearly dinner, or septennial bribe,
Wait on the shore, and, as the waves run high,
On the tost vessel bend their eager eye,
Which to their coast directs its vent'rous way;
Theirs, or the ocean's, miserable prey.   80
    As on their neighbouring beach yon swallows stand,
And wait for favouring winds to leave the land;
While still for flight the ready wing is spread:
So waited I the favouring hour, and fled;
Fled from these shores where guilt and famine reign,   85
And cried, Ah! hapless they who still remain;
Who still remain to hear the ocean roar,
Whose greedy waves devour the lessening shore;
Till some fierce tide, with more imperious sway,
Sweeps the low hut and all it holds away;   90
When the sad tenant weeps from door to door;
And begs a poor protection from the poor!

    Theirs is yon House that holds the parish poor,
Whose walls of mud scarce bear the broken door;
There, where the putrid vapours, flagging, play,   95
And the dull wheel hums doleful through the day; –
There children dwell who know no parents' care;
Parents, who know no children's love, dwell there!
Heart-broken matrons on their joyless bed,
Forsaken wives, and mothers never wed;   100
Dejected widows with unheeded tears,
And crippled age with more than childhood fears;
The lame, the blind, and, far the happiest they!
The moping idiot, and the madman gay.
    Here too the sick their final doom receive,   105
Here brought, amid the scenes of grief, to grieve,
Where the loud groans from some sad chamber flow,
Mixt with the clamours of the crowd below;
Here, sorrowing, they each kindred sorrow scan,
And the cold charities of man to man.   110
Whose laws indeed for ruin'd age provide,

And strong compulsion plucks the scrap from pride;
But still that scrap is bought with many a sigh,
And pride embitters what it can't deny.
     Say, ye, opprest by some fantastic woes,   115
Some jarring nerve that baffles your repose;
Who press the downy couch, while slaves advance
With timid eye to read the distant glance;
Who with sad prayers the weary doctor tease,
To name the nameless ever-new disease;   120
  Who with mock patience dire complaints endure,
  Which real pain and that alone can cure;
  How would ye bear in real pain to lie,
  Despised, neglected, left alone to die?
How would ye bear to draw your latest breath.   125
Where all that's wretched paves the way for death?
    Such is that room which one rude beam divides,
And naked rafters form the sloping sides;
Where the vile bands that bind the thatch are seen,
And lath and mud are all that lie between;   130
  Save one dull pane, that, coarsely patch'd, gives way
  To the rude tempest, yet excludes the day:
  Here, on a matted flock, with dust o'erspread,
  The drooping wretch reclines his languid head;
For him no hand the cordial cup applies,   135
Or wipes the tear that stagnates in his eyes;
No friends with soft discourse his pain beguile,
Or promise hope, till sickness wears a smile.
    But soon a loud and hasty summons calls,
Shakes the thin roof, and echoes round the walls;   140
Anon, a figure enters, quaintly neat,
All pride and business, bustle and conceit;
With looks unalter'd by these scenes of woe,
With speed that, entering, speaks his haste to go,
He bids the gazing throng around him fly,   145
And carries fate and physic in his eye:
A potent quack, long versed in human ills,
Who first insults the victim whom he kills;
Whose murd'rous hand a drowsy Bench protect,
And whose most tender mercy is neglect.   150
    Paid by the parish for attendance here,

He wears contempt upon his sapient sneer;
In haste he seeks the bed where Misery lies,
Impatience mark'd in his averted eyes;
And, some habitual queries hurried o'er,   155
Without reply, he rushes on the door:
His drooping patient, long inured to pain,
And long unheeded, knows remonstrance vain;
He ceases now the feeble help to crave
Of man; and silent sinks into the grave.   160
    But ere his death some pious doubts arise,
Some simple fears, which 'bold bad' men despise;
Fain would he ask the parish priest to prove
His title certain to the joys above:
For this he sends the murmuring nurse, who calls   165
The holy stranger to these dismal walls:
And doth not he, the pious man, appear,
He, 'passing rich with forty pounds a year?'
Ah! no; a shepherd of a different stock,
And far unlike him, feeds this little flock: 170
A jovial youth, who thinks his Sunday's task
As much as God or man can fairly ask;
The rest he gives to loves and labours light,
To fields the morning, and to feasts the night;
None better skill'd the noisy pack to guide,   175
To urge their chase, to cheer them or to chide;
A sportsman keen, he shoots through half the day,
And, skill'd at whist, devotes the night to play:
Then, while such honours bloom around his head,
Shall he sit sadly by the sick man's bed,   180
To raise the hope he feels not, or with zeal
To combat fears that e'en the pious feel?
    Now once again the gloomy scene explore,
Less gloomy now; the bitter hour is o'er,
The man of many sorrows sighs no more. –   185
Up yonder hill, behold how sadly slow
The bier moves winding from the vale below:
There lie the happy dead, from trouble free,
And the glad parish pays the frugal fee:
No more, O Death! thy victim starts to hear   190
Churchwarden stern, or kingly overseer;

No more the farmer claims his humble bow,
Thou art his lord, the best of tyrants thou!
　　Now to the church behold the mourners come,
Sedately torpid and devoutly dumb;   195
The village children now their games suspend,
To see the bier that bears their ancient friend:
For he was one in all their idle sport,
And like a monarch ruled their little court;
The pliant bow he form'd, the flying ball,   200
The bat, the wicket, were his labours all;
Him now they follow to his grave, and stand,
Silent and sad, and gazing, hand in hand;
While bending low, their eager eyes explore
The mingled relics of the parish poor.   205
The bell tolls late, the moping owl flies round,
Fear marks the flight and magnifies the sound;
The busy priest, detain'd by weightier care,
Defers his duty till the day of prayer;
And, waiting long, the crowd retire distrest,   210
To think a poor man's bones should lie unblest.

from **Book Two**

No longer truth, though shown in verse, disdain,
But own the Village Life a life of pain:
I too must yield, that oft amid these woes
Are gleams of transient mirth and hours of sweet repose,
Such as you find on yonder sportive Green,   5
The 'squire's tall gate and churchway-walk between;
Where loitering stray a little tribe of friends,
On a fair Sunday when the sermon ends:
Then rural beaux their best attire put on,
To win their nymphs, as other nymphs are won;   10
While those long wed go plain, and by degrees,
Like other husbands, quit their care to please.
Some of the sermon talk, a sober crowd,
And loudly praise, if it were preach'd aloud;

Some on the labours of the week look round,   15
Feel their own worth, and think their toil renown'd;
While some, whose hopes to no renown extend,
Are only pleased to find their labours end.
   Thus, as their hours glide on, with pleasure fraught,
Their careful masters brood the painful thought;   20
Much in their mind they murmur and lament,
That one fair day should be so idly spent;
And think that Heaven deals hard, to tithe their store
And tax their time for preachers and the poor.
   Yet still, ye humbler friends, enjoy your hour,   25
This is your portion, yet unclaim'd of power;
This is Heaven's gift to weary men oppress'd,
And seems the type of their expected rest:
But yours, alas! are joys that soon decay;
Frail joys, begun and ended with the day;   30
Or yet, while day permits those joys to reign,
The village vices drive them from the plain.
   See the stout churl, in drunken fury great,
Strike the bare bosom of his teeming mate!
His naked vices, rude and unrefined,   35
Exert their open empire o'er the mind;
But can we less the senseless rage despise,
Because the savage acts without disguise?
   Yet here Disguise, the city's vice, is seen,
And Slander steals along and taints the Green: 40
At her approach domestic peace is gone,
Domestic broils at her approach come on;
She to the wife the husband's crime conveys,
She tells the husband when his consort strays;
Her busy tongue, through all the little state,   45
Diffuses doubt, suspicion, and debate;
Peace, tim'rous goddess! quits her old domain,
In sentiment and song content to reign.
   Nor are the nymphs that breathe the rural air
So fair as Cynthia's, nor so chaste as fair: 50
These to the town afford each fresher face,
And the clown's trull receives the peer's embrace;
From whom, should chance again convey her down,
The peer's disease in turn attacks the clown.

Here too the 'squire, or 'squire-like farmer, talk,   55
How round their regions nightly pilferers walk;
How from their ponds the fish are borne, and all
The rip'ning treasures from their lofty wall;
How meaner rivals in their sports delight,
Just right enough to claim a doubtful right;   60
Who take a licence round their fields to stray,
A mongrel race! the poachers of the day.
     And hark! the riots of the Green begin,
That sprang at first from yonder noisy inn;
What time the weekly pay was vanish'd all,   65
And the slow hostess scored the threat'ning wall;
What time they ask'd, their friendly feast to close,
A final cup, and that will make them foes;
When blows ensue that break the arm of toil,
And rustic battle ends the boobies' broil.   70
     Save when to yonder Hall they bend their way,
Where the grave Justice ends the grievous fray;
He who recites, to keep the poor in awe,
The law's vast volume – for he knows the law: –
To him with anger or with shame repair   75
The injured peasant and deluded fair.
     Lo! at his throne the silent nymph appears,
Frail by her shape, but modest in her tears;
And while she stands abash'd, with conscious eye,
Some favourite female of her judge glides by,   80
Who views with scornful glance the strumpet's fate,
And thanks the stars that make her keeper great:
Near her the swain, about to bear for life
One certain evil, doubts 'twixt war and wife;
But, while the falt'ring damsel takes her oath,   85
Consents to wed, and so secures them both.
     Yet why, you ask, these humble crimes relate,
Why make the Poor as guilty as the Great?
To show the great, those mightier sons of pride,
How near in vice the lowest are allied;   90
Such are their natures and their passions such,
But these disguise too little, those too much:
So shall the man of power and pleasure see
In his own slave as vile a wretch as he;

In his luxurious lord the servant find   95
His own low pleasures and degenerate mind:
And each in all the kindred vices trace,
Of a poor, blind, bewilder'd, erring race,
Who, a short time in varied fortune past,
Die, and are equal in the dust at last.   100
    And you, ye Poor, who still lament your fate,
Forbear to envy those you call the Great;
And know, amid those blessings they possess,
They are, like you, the victims of distress;
While Sloth with many a pang torments her slave,   105
Fear waits on guilt, and Danger shakes the brave.

from **The Newspaper**

A time like this, a busy, bustling time,
Suits ill with writers, very ill with rhyme:
Unheard we sing, when party-rage runs strong,
And mightier madness checks the flowing song:
Or, should we force the peaceful Muse to wield   5
Her feeble arms amid the furious field,
Where party-pens a wordy war maintain,
Poor is her anger, and her friendship vain;
And oft the foes who feel her sting, combine,
Till serious vengeance pays an idle line: 10
For party-poets are like wasps, who dart
Death to themselves, and to their foes but smart.
    Hard then our fate: if general themes we choose,
Neglect awaits the song, and chills the Muse;
Or should we sing the subject of the day,   15
To-morrow's wonder puffs our praise away.
More blest the bards of that poetic time,
When all found readers who could find a rhyme;
Green grew the bays on every teeming head,
And Cibber was enthroned, and Settle read.   20
Sing, drooping Muse, the cause of thy decline;

Why reign no more the once-triumphant Nine?
Alas! new charms the wavering many gain,
And rival sheets the reader's eye detain;
A daily swarm, that banish every Muse,   25
Come flying forth, and mortals call them News:
For these, unread, the noblest volumes lie;
For these, in sheets unsoil'd, the Muses die;
Unbought, unblest, the virgin copies wait
In vain for fame, and sink, unseen, to fate.   30
     Since, then, the Town forsakes us for our foes,
The smoothest numbers for the harshest prose;
Let us, with generous scorn, the taste deride,
And sing our rivals with a rival's pride.
     Ye gentle poets, who so oft complain   35
That foul neglect is all your labours gain;
That pity only checks your growing spite
To erring man, and prompts you still to write;
That your choice works on humble stalls are laid,
Or vainly grace the windows of the trade;   40
Be ye my friends, if friendship e'er can warm
Those rival bosoms whom the Muses charm:
Think of the common cause wherein we go,
Like gallant Greeks against the Trojan foe;
Nor let one peevish chief his leader blame,   45
Till, crown'd with conquest, we regain our fame;
And let us join our forces to subdue
This bold assuming but successful crew.
     I sing of News, and all those vapid sheets
The rattling hawker vends through gaping streets;   50
Whate'er their name, whate'er the time they fly,
Damp from the press, to charm the reader's eye:
For, soon as Morning dawns with roseate hue,
The Herald of the morn arises too;
Post after Post succeeds, and, all day long,   55
Gazette and Ledgers swarm, a noisy throng.
When evening comes, she comes with all her train
Of Ledgers, Chronicles, and Posts again,
Like bats, appearing, when the sun goes down,
From holes obscure and corners of the town.   60
Of all these triflers, all like these, I write;

Oh! like my subject could my song delight,
The crowd at Lloyd's one poet's name should raise,
And all the Alley echo to his praise.
   In shoals the hours their constant numbers bring,   65
Like insects waking to th' advancing spring;
Which take their rise from grubs obscene that lie
In shallow pools, or thence ascend the sky:
Such are these base ephemeras, so born
To die before the next revolving morn.   70
   Yet thus they differ: insect-tribes are lost
In the first visit of a winter's frost;
While these remain, a base but constant breed,
Whose swarming sons their short-lived sires succeed;
No changing season makes their number less,   75
Nor Sunday shines a sabbath on the press!
   Then lo! the sainted Monitor is born,
Whose pious face some sacred texts adorn:
As artful sinners cloak the secret sin,
To veil with seeming grace the guile within;   80
So Moral Essays on his front appear,
But all is carnal business in the rear;
The fresh-coin'd lie, the secret whisper'd last,
And all the gleanings of the six days past.
   With these retired, through half the Sabbath day,   85
The London lounger yawns his hours away:
Not so, my little flock! your preacher fly,
Nor waste the time no worldly wealth can buy;
But let the decent maid and sober clown
Pray for these idlers of the sinful town: 90
This day, at least, on nobler themes bestow,
Nor give to Woodfall, or the world below.
   But, Sunday past, what numbers flourish then,
What wondrous labours of the press and pen!
Diurnal most, some thrice each week affords,   95
Some only once, – O avarice of words!
When thousand starving minds such manna seek,
To drop the precious food but once a week.
   Endless it were to sing the powers of all,
Their names, their numbers; how they rise and fall: 100
Like baneful herbs the gazer's eye they seize,

Rush to the head, and poison where they please:
Like idle flies, a busy, buzzing train,
They drop their maggots in the trifler's brain:
That genial soil receives the fruitful store,   105
And there they grow, and breed a thousand more.

The Parish Register

from **Part Two: Marriages**

Sir Edward Archer is an amorous knight,
And maidens chaste and lovely shun his sight;
His bailiff's daughter suited much his taste,
For Fanny Price was lovely and was chaste;
To her the Knight with gentle looks drew near,   5
And timid voice assumed, to banish fear: –
  'Hope of my life, dear sovereign of my breast,
Which, since I knew thee, knows not joy nor rest;
Know, thou art all that my delighted eyes,
My fondest thoughts, my proudest wishes prize;   10
And is that bosom – (what on earth so fair!)
To cradle some coarse peasant's sprawling heir,
To be that pillow which some surly swain
May treat with scorn and agonise with pain?
Art thou, sweet maid, a ploughman's wants to share,   15
To dread his insult, to support his care;
To hear his follies, his contempt to prove,
And (oh! the torment!) to endure his love;
Till want and deep regret those charms destroy,
That time would spare, if time were pass'd in joy?   20
With him, in varied pains, from morn till night,
Your hours shall pass; yourself a ruffian's right;
Your softest bed shall be the knotted wool;
Your purest drink the waters of the pool;
Your sweetest food will but your life sustain,   25
And your best pleasure be a rest from pain;
While, through each year, as health and strength abate,
You'll weep your woes and wonder at your fate;
And cry, "Behold," as life's last cares come on,
"My burthens growing when my strength is gone."   30
  'Now turn with me, and all the young desire,
That taste can form, that fancy can require;

All that excites enjoyment, or procures
Wealth, health, respect, delight, and love, are yours:
Sparkling, in cups of gold, your wines shall flow,   35
Grace that fair hand, in that dear bosom glow;
Fruits of each clime, and flowers, through all the year,
Shall on your walls and in your walks appear:
Where all beholding, shall your praise repeat,
No fruit so tempting and no flower so sweet: 40
The softest carpets in your rooms shall lie,
Pictures of happiest loves shall meet your eye,
And tallest mirrors, reaching to the floor,
Shall show you all the object I adore;
Who, by the hands of wealth and fashion dress'd,   45
By slaves attended and by friends caress'd,
Shall move, a wonder, through the public ways,
And hear the whispers of adoring praise.
Your female friends, though gayest of the gay,
Shall see you happy, and shall, sighing, say,   50
While smother'd envy rises in the breast, –
"Oh! that we lived so beauteous and so blest!"
   'Come, then, my mistress, and my wife; for she
Who trusts my honour is the wife for me;
Your slave, your husband, and your friend employ,   55
In search of pleasures we may both enjoy.'
To this the Damsel, meekly firm, replied:
'My mother loved, was married, toil'd, and died;
With joys, she'd griefs, had troubles in her course,
But not one grief was pointed by remorse;   60
My mind is fix'd, to Heaven I resign,
And be her love, her life, her comforts mine.'
   Tyrants have wept; and those with hearts of steel,
Unused the anguish of the heart to heal,
Have yet the transient power of virtue known,   65
And felt th' imparted joy promote their own.
   Our Knight relenting, now befriends a youth,
Who to the yielding maid had vow'd his truth:
And finds in that fair deed a sacred joy,
That will not perish, and that cannot cloy; –   70
A living joy, that shall its spirit keep,
When every beauty fades, and all the passions sleep.

from **Part Three: Burials**

Down by the church-way walk, and where the brook
Winds round the chancel like a shepherd's crook;
In that small house, with those green pales before,
Where jasmine trails on either side the door;
Where those dark shrubs, that now grow wild at will,   5
Were clipp'd in form and tantalised with skill;
Where cockles blanch'd and pebbles neatly spread,
Form'd shining borders for the larkspurs' bed; –
There lived a lady, wise, austere, and nice,
Who show'd her virtue by her scorn of vice;   10
In the dear fashions of her youth she dress'd,
A pea-green Joseph was her favourite vest;
Erect she stood, she walk'd with stately mien,
Tight was her length of stays, and she was tall and lean.
There long she lived in maiden-state immured,   15
From looks of love and treacherous man secured;
Though evil fame – (but that was long before)
Had blown her dubious blast at Catherine's door:
A Captain thither, rich from India came,
And though a *cousin* call'd, it touch'd her fame: 20
Her annual stipend rose from his behest,
And all the long-prized treasures she possess'd: –
If aught like joy awhile appear'd to stay
In that stern face, and chase those frowns away;
'T was when her treasures she disposed for view,   25
And heard the praises to their splendour due;
Silks beyond price, so rich, they'd stand alone,
And diamonds blazing on the buckled zone;
Rows of rare pearls by curious workmen set,
And bracelets fair in box of glossy jet;   30
Bright polish'd amber precious from its size,
Or forms the fairest fancy could devise:
Her drawers of cedar, shut with secret springs,
Conceal'd the watch of gold and rubied rings;
Letters, long proofs of love, and verses fine   35
Round the pink'd rims of crisped Valentine.

Her china-closet, cause of daily care,
For woman's wonder held her pencill'd ware;
That pictured wealth of China and Japan,
Like its cold mistress, shunn'd the eye of man.   40
   Her neat small room, adorn'd with maiden-taste,
A clipp'd French puppy, first of favourites, graced:
A parrot next, but dead and stuff'd with art;
(For Poll, when living, lost the Lady's heart,
And then his life; for he was heard to speak   45
Such frightful words as tinged his Lady's cheek:)
Unhappy bird! who had no power to prove,
Save by such speech, his gratitude and love.
A grey old cat his whiskers lick'd beside;
A type of sadness in the house of pride.   50
The polish'd surface of an India chest,
A glassy globe, in frame of ivory, press'd;
Where swam two finny creatures; one of gold,
Of silver one; both beauteous to behold: –
All these were form'd the guiding taste to suit;   55
The beast well-manner'd and the fishes mute.
A widow'd Aunt was there, compell'd by need
The nymph to flatter and her tribe to feed;
Who, veiling well her scorn, endured the clog,
Mute as the fish and fawning as the dog.   60
   As years increased, these treasures, her delight,
Arose in value in their owner's sight:
A miser knows that, view it as he will,
A guinea kept is but a guinea still:
And so he puts it to its proper use,   65
That something more this guinea may produce;
But silks and rings, in the possessor's eyes,
The oft'ner seen, the more in value rise,
And thus are wisely hoarded to bestow
The kind of pleasure that with years will grow.   70
   But what avail'd their worth – if worth had they –
In the sad summer of her slow decay?
   Then we beheld her turn an anxious look
From trunks and chests, and fix it on her book, –
A rich-bound Book of Prayer the Captain gave,   75
(Some Princess had it, or was said to have;)

And then once more, on all her stores, look round,
And draw a sigh so piteous and profound,
That told, 'Alas! how hard from these to part,
And for new hopes and habits form the heart!   80
What shall I do (she cried), my peace of mind
To gain in dying, and to die resign'd?'
   'Hear,' we return'd; – 'these baubles cast aside,
Nor give thy God a rival in thy pride;
Thy closets shut, and ope thy kitchen's door;   85
There own thy failings, *here* invite the poor;
A friend of Mammon let thy bounty make;
For widow's prayers, thy vanities forsake;
And let the hungry, of thy pride partake:
Then shall thy inward eye with joy survey   90
The angel Mercy tempering Death's delay!'
Alas! 't was hard; the treasures still had charms,
Hope still its flattery, sickness its alarms;
Still was the same unsettled, clouded view,
And the same plaintive cry, 'What shall I do?'   95
   Nor change appear'd; for when her race was run,
Doubtful we all exclaim'd, 'What has been done?'
Apart she lived, and still she lies alone;
Yon earthy heap awaits the flattering stone,
On which invention shall be long employ'd,   100
To show the various worth of Catherine Lloyd.

The Borough

General Description

'Describe the Borough' – though our idle tribe
May love description, can we so describe,
That you shall fairly streets and buildings trace,
And all that gives distinction to a place?
This cannot be; yet, moved by your request,   5
A part I paint – let Fancy form the rest.
  Cities and towns, the various haunts of men,
Require the pencil; they defy the pen:
Could he, who sang so well the Grecian fleet,
So well have sung of alley, lane, or street?   10
Can measured lines these various buildings show,
The Town-Hall Turning, or the Prospect Row?
Can I the seats of wealth and want explore,
And lengthen out my lays from door to door?
  Then let thy Fancy aid me – I repair   15
From this tall mansion of our last-year's Mayor,
Till we the outskirts of the Borough reach,
And these half-buried buildings next the beach;
Where hang at open doors the net and cork,
While squalid sea-dames mend the meshy work;   20
Till comes the hour, when fishing through the tide,
The weary husband throws his freight aside;
A living mass, which now demands the wife,
Th' alternate labours of their humble life.
  Can scenes like these withdraw thee from thy wood,   25
Thy upland forest or thy valley's flood?
Seek then thy garden's shrubby bound, and look,
As it steals by, upon the bordering brook;
That winding streamlet, limpid, lingering, slow,
Where the reeds whisper when the zephyrs blow;   30
Where in the midst, upon her throne of green,
Sits the large Lily as the water's queen;

And makes the current, forced awhile to stay,
Murmur and bubble as it shoots away;
Draw then the strongest contrast to that stream,   35
And our broad river will before thee seem.
　　With ceaseless motion comes and goes the tide,
Flowing, it fills the channel vast and wide;
Then back to sea, with strong majestic sweep
It rolls, in ebb yet terrible and deep;   40
Here Samphire-banks and Salt-wort bound the flood,
There stakes the sea-weeds withering on the mud;
And higher up, a ridge of all things base,
Which some strong tide has roll'd upon the place.
　　Thy gentle river boasts its pigmy boat,   45
Urged on by pains, half grounded, half afloat;
While at her stern an angler takes his stand,
And marks the fish he purposes to land;
From that clear space, where, in the cheerful ray
Of the warm sun, the scaly people play.   50
　　Far other craft our prouder river shows,
Hoys, pinks and sloops; brigs, brigantines and snows:
Nor angler we on our wide stream descry,
But one poor dredger where his oysters lie:
He, cold and wet, and driving with the tide,   55
Beats his weak arms against his tarry side,
Then drains the remnant of diluted gin,
To aid the warmth that languishes within;
Renewing oft his poor attempts to beat
His tingling fingers into gathering heat.   60
　　He shall again be seen when evening comes,
And social parties crowd their favourite rooms:
Where on the table pipes and papers lie,
The steaming bowl or foaming tankard by;
'T is then, with all these comforts spread around,   65
They hear the painful dredger's welcome sound;
And few themselves the savoury boon deny,
The food that feeds, the living luxury.
　　Yon is our Quay! those smaller hoys from town,
Its various ware, for country-use, bring down;   70
Those laden waggons, in return, impart
The country-produce to the city mart;

Hark! to the clamour in that miry road,
Bounded and narrow'd by yon vessel's load;
The lumbering wealth she empties round the place,   75
Package, and parcel, hogshead, chest, and case:
While the loud seaman and the angry hind,
Mingling in business, bellow to the wind.
    Near these a crew amphibious, in the docks,
Rear, for the sea, those castles on the stocks: 80
See! the long keel, which soon the waves must hide;
See! the strong ribs which form the roomy side;
Bolts yielding slowly to the sturdiest stroke,
And planks which curve and crackle in the smoke.
Around the whole rise cloudy wreaths, and far   85
Bear the warm pungence of o'er-boiling tar.
    Dabbling on shore half-naked sea-boys crowd,
Swim round a ship, or swing upon the shroud;
Or in a boat purloin'd, with paddles play,
And grow familiar with the watery way: 90
Young though they be, they feel whose sons they are,
They know what British seamen do and dare;
Proud of that fame, they raise and they enjoy
The rustic wonder of the village-boy.
    Before you bid these busy scenes adieu,   95
Behold the wealth that lies in public view,
Those far-extended heaps of coal and coke,
Where fresh-fill'd lime-kilns breathe their stifling smoke.
This shall pass off, and you behold, instead,
The night-fire gleaming on its chalky bed;   100
When from the Light-house brighter beams will rise,
To show the shipman where the shallow lies.
    Thy walks are ever pleasant; every scene
Is rich in beauty, lively, or serene –
Rich – is that varied view with woods around,   105
Seen from the seat, within the shrubb'ry bound;
Where shines the distant lake, and where appear
From ruins bolting, unmolested deer;
Lively – the village-green, the inn, the place,
Where the good widow schools her infant-race.   110
Shops, whence are heard the hammer and the saw,
And village pleasures unreproved by law:

Then how serene! when in your favourite room,
Gales from your jasmines soothe the evening gloom;
When from your upland paddock you look down,   115
And just perceive the smoke which hides the town;
When weary peasants at the close of day
Walk to their cots, and part upon the way;
When cattle slowly cross the shallow brook,
And shepherds pen their folds, and rest upon their crook.   120
    We prune our hedges, prime our slender trees,
And nothing looks untutor'd and at ease,
On the wide heath, or in the flow'ry vale,
We scent the vapours of the sea-born gale;
Broad-beaten paths lead on from stile to stile,   125
And sewers from streets, the road-side banks defile;
Our guarded fields a sense of danger sow,
Where garden-crops with corn and clover grow;
Fences are form'd of wreck and placed around,
(With tenters tipp'd) a strong repulsive bound;   130
Wide and deep ditches by the gardens run,
And there in ambush lie the trap and gun;
Or yon broad board, which guards each tempting prize,
'Like a tall bully, lifts its head and lies.'
    There stands a cottage with an open door,   135
Its garden undefended blooms before:
Her wheel is still, and overturn'd her stool,
While the lone Widow seeks the neighb'ring pool:
This gives us hope, all views of town to shun –
No! here are tokens of the Sailor-son;   140
That old blue jacket, and that shirt of check,
And silken kerchief for the seaman's neck;
Sea-spoils and shells from many a distant shore,
And furry robe from frozen Labrador.
    Our busy streets and sylvan-walks between,   145
Fen, marshes, bog and heath all intervene;
Here pits of crag, with spongy, plashy base,
To some enrich th' uncultivated space:
For there are blossoms rare, and curious rush,
The gale's rich balm, and sun-dew's crimson blush   150
Whose velvet leaf with radiant beauty dress'd,
Forms a gay pillow for the plover's breast.

Not distant far, a house commodious made,
(Lonely yet public stands) for Sunday-trade;
Thither, for this day free, gay parties go,   155
Their tea-house walk, their tippling rendezvous;
There humble couples sit in corner-bowers,
Or gaily ramble for th' allotted hours;
Sailors and lasses from the town attend,
The servant-lover, the apprentice-friend;   160
With all the idle social tribes who seek
And find their humble pleasures once a week.
    Turn to the watery world! – but who to thee
(A wonder yet unview'd) shall paint – the Sea?
Various and vast, sublime in all its forms,   165
When lull'd by zephyrs, or when roused by storms,
Its colours changing, when from clouds and sun
Shades after shades upon the surface run;
Embrown'd and horrid now, and now serene,
In limpid blue, and evanescent green;   170
And oft the foggy banks on ocean lie,
Lift the fair sail, and cheat th' experienced eye.
    Be it the Summer-noon: a sandy space
The ebbing tide has left upon its place;
Then just the hot and stony beach above,   175
Light twinkling streams in bright confusion move;
(For heated thus, the warmer air ascends,
And with the cooler in its fall contends) –
Then the broad bosom of the ocean keeps
An equal motion; swelling as it sleeps,   180
Then slowly sinking; curling to the strand,
Faint, lazy waves o'ercreep the ridgy sand,
Or tap the tarry boat with gentle blow,
And back return in silence, smooth and slow.
Ships in the calm seem anchor'd; for they glide   185
On the still sea, urged solely by the tide:
Art thou not present, this calm scene before,
Where all beside is pebbly length of shore,
And far as eye can reach, it can discern no more?
    Yet sometimes comes a ruffling cloud to make   190
The quiet surface of the ocean shake;
As an awaken'd giant with a frown

Might show his wrath, and then to sleep sink down.
   View now the Winter-storm! above, one cloud,
Black and unbroken, all the skies o'ershroud;   195
Th' unwieldy porpoise through the day before
Had roll'd in view of boding men on shore;
And sometimes hid and sometimes show'd his form,
Dark as the cloud, and furious as the storm.
   All where the eye delights, yet dreads to roam,   200
The breaking billows cast the flying foam
Upon the billows rising – all the deep
Is restless change; the waves so swell'd and steep,
Breaking and sinking, and the sunken swells,
Nor one, one moment, in its station dwells: 205
But nearer land you may the billows trace,
As if contending in their watery chase;
May watch the mightiest till the shoal they reach,
Then break and hurry to their utmost stretch;
Curl'd as they come, they strike with furious force,   210
And then re-flowing, take their grating course,
Raking the rounded flints, which ages past
Roll'd by their rage, and shall to ages last.
   Far off the Petrel in the troubled way
Swims with her brood, or flutters in the spray;   215
She rises often, often drops again,
And sports at ease on the tempestuous main.
   High o'er the restless deep, above the reach
Of gunner's hope, vast flights of Wild-ducks stretch;
Far as the eye can glance on either side,   220
In a broad space and level line they glide;
All in their wedge-like figures from the north,
Day after day, flight after flight, go forth.
   In-shore their passage tribes of Sea-gulls urge,
And drop for prey within the sweeping surge;   225
Oft in the rough opposing blast they fly
Far back, then turn, and all their force apply,
While to the storm they give their weak complaining cry;
Or clap the sleek white pinion to the breast,
And in the restless ocean dip for rest.   230
   Darkness begins to reign; the louder wind
Appals the weak and awes the firmer mind;

But frights not him, whom evening and the spray
In part conceal – yon Prowler on his way:
Lo! he has something seen; he runs apace,   235
As if he fear'd companion in the chase;
He sees his prize, and now he turns again,
Slowly and sorrowing – 'Was your search in vain?'
Gruffly he answers, ''T is a sorry sight!
A seaman's body: there'll be more to-night!'   240
      Hark! to those sounds! they're from distress at sea:
How quick they come! What terrors may there be!
Yes, 't is a driven vessel: I discern
Lights, signs of terror, gleaming from the stern;
Others behold them too, and from the town   245
In various parties seamen hurry down;
Their wives pursue, and damsels urged by dread,
Lest men so dear be into danger led;
Their head the gown has hooded, and their call
In this sad night is piercing like the squall;   250
They feel their kinds of power, and when they meet,
Chide, fondle, weep, dare, threaten, or intreat.
      See one poor girl, all terror and alarm,
Has fondly seized upon her lover's arm;
'Thou shalt not venture,' and he answers 'No!   255
I will not' – still she cries, 'Thou shalt not go.'
      No need of this; not here the stoutest boat
Can through such breakers, o'er such billows float,
Yet may they view these lights upon the beach,
Which yield them hope, whom help can never reach.   260
      From parted clouds the moon her radiance throws
On the wild waves, and all the danger shows;
But shows them beaming in her shining vest,
Terrific splendour! gloom in glory dress'd!
This for a moment, and then clouds again   265
Hide every beam, and fear and darkness reign.
      But hear we now those sounds? Do lights appear?
I see them not! the storm alone I hear:
And lo! the sailors homeward take their way;
Man must endure – let us submit and pray.   270
      Such are our Winter-views: but night comes on –
Now business sleeps, and daily cares are gone;

Now parties form, and some their friends assist
To waste the idle hours at sober whist;
The tavern's pleasure or the concert's charm   275
Unnumber'd moments of their sting disarm;
Play-bills and open doors a crowd invite,
To pass off one dread portion of the night;
And show and song and luxury combined,
Lift off from man this burthen of mankind.   280
   Others advent'rous walk abroad and meet
Returning parties pacing through the street,
When various voices, in the dying day,
Hum in our walks, and greet us in our way;
When tavern-lights flit on from room to room,   285
And guide the tippling sailor staggering home:
There as we pass, the jingling bells betray
How business rises with the closing day:
Now walking silent, by the river's side,
The ear perceives the rippling of the tide;   290
Or measured cadence of the lads who tow
Some enter'd hoy, to fix her in her row;
Or hollow sound, which from the parish-bell
To some departed spirit bids farewell!
   Thus shall you something of our Borough know,   295
Far as a verse, with Fancy's aid, can show;
Of Sea or River, of a Quay or Street,
The best description must be incomplete;
But when a happier theme succeeds, and when
Men are our subjects and the deeds of men;   300
Then may we find the Muse in happier style,
And we may sometimes sigh and sometimes smile.

Peter Grimes

Old Peter Grimes made fishing his employ,
His wife he cabin'd with him and his boy,
And seem'd that life laborious to enjoy:
To town came quiet Peter with his fish,
And had of all a civil word and wish.   5
He left his trade upon the Sabbath-day,
And took young Peter in his hand to pray:
But soon the stubborn boy from care broke loose,
At first refused, then added his abuse:
His father's love he scorn'd, his power defied,   10
But being drunk, wept sorely when he died.
    Yes! then he wept, and to his mind there came
Much of his conduct, and he felt the shame, –
How he had oft the good old man reviled,
And never paid the duty of a child;   15
How, when the father in his Bible read,
He in contempt and anger left the shed:
'It is the word of life,' the parent cried;
– 'This is the life itself,' the boy replied;
And while old Peter in amazement stood,   20
Gave the hot spirit to his boiling blood:–
How he, with oath and furious speech, began
To prove his freedom and assert the man;
And when the parent check'd his impious rage,
How he had cursed the tyranny of age, –   25
Nay, once had dealt the sacrilegious blow
On his bare head, and laid his parent low;
The father groan'd – 'If thou art old,' said he,
'And hast a son – thou wilt remember me:
Thy mother left me in a happy time,   30
Thou kill'dst not her – Heav'n spares the double crime.'
    On an inn-settle, in his maudlin grief,
This he revolved, and drank for his relief.
    Now lived the youth in freedom, but debarr'd
From constant pleasure, and he thought it hard;   35
Hard that he could not every wish obey,

But must awhile relinquish ale and play;
Hard! that he could not to his cards attend,
But must acquire the money he would spend.
    With greedy eye he look'd on all he saw,   40
He knew not justice, and he laugh'd at law;
On all he mark'd, he stretch'd his ready hand;
He fish'd by water and he filch'd by land:
Oft in the night has Peter dropp'd his oar,
Fled from his boat, and sought for prey on shore;   45
Oft up the hedge-row glided, on his back
Bearing the orchard's produce in a sack,
Or farm-yard load, tugg'd fiercely from the stack;
And as these wrongs to greater numbers rose,
The more he look'd on all men as his foes.   50
    He built a mud-wall'd hovel, where he kept
His various wealth, and there he oft-times slept;
But no success could please his cruel soul,
He wish'd for one to trouble and control;
He wanted some obedient boy to stand   55
And bear the blow of his outrageous hand;
And hoped to find in some propitious hour
A feeling creature subject to his power.
    Peter had heard there were in London then, –
Still have they being! – workhouse-clearing men,   60
Who, undisturb'd by feelings just or kind,
Would parish-boys to needy tradesmen bind:
They in their want a trifling sum would take,
And toiling slaves of piteous orphans make.
    Such Peter sought, and when a lad was found,   65
The sum was dealt him, and the slave was bound.
Some few in town observed in Peter's trap
A boy, with jacket blue and woollen cap;
But none enquired how Peter used the rope,
Or what the bruise, that made the stripling stoop;   70
None could the ridges on his back behold,
None sought him shiv'ring in the winter's cold;
None put the question, – 'Peter, dost thou give
The boy his food? – What, man! the lad must live:
Consider, Peter, let the child have bread,   75
He'll serve thee better if he's stroked and fed.'

None reason'd thus – and some, on hearing cries,
Said calmly, 'Grimes is at his exercise.'
  Pinn'd, beaten, cold, pinch'd, threatened, and abused –
His efforts punish'd and his food refused, –   80
Awake tormented, – soon aroused from sleep, –
Struck if he wept, and yet compell'd to weep,
The trembling boy dropp'd down and strove to pray,
Received a blow, and trembling turn'd away,
Or sobb'd and hid his piteous face; – while he,   85
The savage master, grinn'd in horrid glee:
He'd now the power he ever loved to show,
A feeling being subject to his blow.
  Thus lived the lad, in hunger, peril, pain,
His tears despised, his supplications vain: 90
Compell'd by fear to lie, by need to steal,
His bed uneasy and unbless'd his meal,
For three sad years the boy his tortures bore,
And then his pains and trials were no more.
  'How died he, Peter?' when the people said,   95
He growl'd – 'I found him lifeless in his bed,'
Then tried for softer tone, and sigh'd, 'Poor Sam is dead.'
Yet murmurs were there, and some questions ask'd –
How he was fed, how punish'd, and how task'd?
Much they suspected, but they litle proved,   100
And Peter pass'd untroubled and unmoved.
  Another boy with equal ease was found,
The money granted, and the victim bound;
And what his fate? – One night it chanced he fell
From the boat's mast and perish'd in her well,   105
Where fish were living kept, and where the boy
(So reason'd men) could not himself destroy:–
  'Yes! so it was,' said Peter, 'in his play,
(For he was idle both by night and day,)
He climb'd the main-mast and then fell below;' –   110
Then show'd his corpse, and pointed to the blow:
'What said the jury?' – they were long in doubt,
But sturdy Peter faced the matter out:
So they dismiss'd him, saying at the time,
'Keep fast your hatchway when you've boys who climb.'   115
This hit the conscience, and he colour'd more

Than for the closest questions put before.
    Thus all his fears the verdict set aside,
And at the slave-shop Peter still applied.
    Then came a boy, of manners soft and mild, –   120
Our seamen's wives with grief beheld the child;
All thought (the poor themselves) that he was one
Of gentle blood, some noble sinner's son,
Who had, belike, deceived some humble maid,
Whom he had first seduced and then betray'd: –   125
However this, he seem'd a gracious lad,
In grief submissive and with patience sad.
    Passive he labour'd, till his slender frame
Bent with his loads, and he at length was lame:
Strange that a frame so weak could bear so long   130
The grossest insult and the foulest wrong;
But there were causes – in the town they gave
Fire, food, and comfort, to the gentle slave;
And though stern Peter, with a cruel hand,
And knotted rope, enforced the rude command,   135
Yet he consider'd what he'd lately felt,
And his vile blows with selfish pity dealt.
    One day such draughts the cruel fisher made,
He could not vend them in his borough-trade,
But sail'd for London-mart: the boy was ill,   140
But ever humbled to his master's will;
And on the river, where they smoothly sail'd,
He strove with terror and awhile prevail'd;
But new to danger on the angry sea,
He clung affrighten'd to his master's knee: 145
The boat grew leaky and the wind was strong,
Rough was the passage and the time was long;
His liquor fail'd, and Peter's wrath arose, –
No more is known – the rest we must suppose,
Or learn of Peter: – Peter says, he 'spied   150
The stripling's danger and for harbour tried;
Meantime the fish, and then th' apprentice died.'
    The pitying women raised a clamour round,
And weeping said, 'Thou hast thy 'prentice drown'd.'
    Now the stern man was summon'd to the hall,   155
To tell his tale before the burghers all:

He gave th' account; profess'd the lad he loved,
And kept his brazen features all unmoved.
    The mayor himself with tone severe replied, –
'Henceforth with thee shall never boy abide;   160
Hire thee a freeman, whom thou durst not beat,
But who, in thy despite, will sleep and eat:
Free thou art now! – again shouldst thou appear,
Thou'lt find thy sentence, like thy soul, severe.'
    Alas! for Peter not a helping hand,   165
So was he hated, could he now command;
Alone he row'd his boat, alone he cast
His nets beside, or made his anchor fast;
To hold a rope or hear a curse was none, –
He toil'd and rail'd; he groan'd and swore alone.   170
    Thus by himself compell'd to live each day,
To wait for certain hours the tide's delay;
At the same time the same dull views to see,
The bounding marsh-bank and the blighted tree;
The water only, when the tides were high,   175
When low the mud half-cover'd and half-dry;
The sun-burnt tar that blisters on the planks,
And bank-side stakes in their uneven ranks;
Heaps of entangled weeds that slowly float,
As the tide rolls by the impeded boat.   180
    When tides were neap, and, in the sultry day,
Through the tall bounding mud-banks made their way,
Which on each side rose swelling, and below
The dark warm flood ran silently and slow;
There anchoring, Peter chose from man to hide,   185
There hang his head, and view the lazy tide
In its hot slimy channel slowly glide;
Where the small eels that left the deeper way
For the warm shore, within the shallows play;
Where gaping muscles, left upon the mud,   190
Slope their slow passage to the fallen flood; –
Here dull and hopeless he'd lie down and trace
How sidelong crabs had scrawl'd their crooked race;
Or sadly listen to the tuneless cry
Of fishing gull or clanging golden-eye;   195
What time the sea-birds to the marsh would come,

And the loud bittern, from the bull-rush home,
Gave from the salt-ditch side the bellowing boom:
He nursed the feelings these dull scenes produce,
And loved to stop beside the opening sluice;   200
Where the small stream, confined in narrow bound,
Ran with a dull, unvaried, sadd'ning sound;
Where all, presented to the eye or ear,
Oppress'd the soul with misery, grief, and fear.
 Besides these objects, there were places three,   205
Which Peter seem'd with certain dread to see;
When he drew near them he would turn from each,
And loudly whistle till he pass'd the reach.
 A change of scene to him brought no relief,
In town, 't was plain, men took him for a thief: 210
The sailors' wives would stop him in the street,
And say, 'Now, Peter, thou'st no boy to beat:'
Infants at play, when they perceived him, ran,
Warning each other – 'That's the wicked man:'
He growl'd an oath, and in an angry tone   215
Cursed the whole place and wish'd to be alone.
 Alone he was, the same dull scenes in view,
And still more gloomy in his sight they grew:
Though man he hated, yet employ'd alone
At bootless labour, he would swear and groan,   220
Cursing the shoals that glided by the spot,
And gulls that caught them when his arts could not.
 Cold nervous tremblings shook his sturdy frame,
And strange disease – he couldn't say the name;
Wild were his dreams, and oft he rose in fright,   225
Waked by his view of horrors in the night, –
Horrors that would the sternest minds amaze,
Horrors that demons might be proud to raise:
And though he felt forsaken, grieved at heart,
To think he lived from all mankind apart;   230
Yet, if a man approach'd, in terrors he would start.
 A winter pass'd since Peter saw the town,
And summer lodgers were again come down;
These, idly curious, with their glasses spied
The ships in bay as anchor'd for the tide, –   235
The river's craft, – the bustle of the quay, –

And sea-port views, which landmen love to see.
   One, up the river, had a man and boat
Seen day by day, now anchor'd, now afloat;
Fisher he seem'd, yet used no net nor hook;   240
Of sea-fowl swimming by no heed he took,
But on the gliding waves still fix'd his lazy look:
At certain stations he would view the stream,
As if he stood bewildered in a dream,
Or that some power had chain'd him for a time,   245
To feel a curse or meditate on crime.
   This known, some curious, some in pity went,
And others question'd – 'Wretch, dost thou repent?'
He heard, he trembled, and in fear resign'd
His boat: new terror fill'd his restless mind;   250
Furious he grew, and up the country ran,
And there they seized him – a distemper'd man: –
Him we received, and to a parish-bed,
Follow'd and cursed, the groaning man was led.
   Here when they saw him, whom they used to shun,   255
A lost, lone man, so harass'd and undone;
Our gentle females, ever prompt to feel,
Perceived compassion on their anger steal;
His crimes they could not from their memories blot,
But they were grieved, and trembled at his lot.   260
   A Priest too came, to whom his words are told;
And all the signs they shudder'd to behold.
   'Look! look!' they cried; 'his limbs with horror shake,
And as he grinds his teeth, what noise they make!
How glare his angry eyes, and yet he's not awake: 265
See! what cold drops upon his forehead stand,
And how he clenches that broad bony hand.'
   The Priest attending, found he spoke at times
As one alluding to his fears and crimes;
'It was the fall,' he mutter'd, 'I can show   270
The manner how, – I never struck a blow:' –
And then aloud, – 'Unhand me, free my chain;
On oath he fell – it struck him to the brain: –
Why ask my father? – that old man will swear
Against my life; besides, he wasn't there: –   275
What, all agreed? – Am I to die to-day? –

My Lord, in mercy give me time to pray.'
   Then as they watch'd him, calmer he became,
And grew so weak he couldn't move his frame,
But murmuring spake – while they could see and hear   280
The start of terror and the groan of fear;
See the large dew-beads on his forehead rise,
And the cold death-drop glaze his sunken eyes,
Nor yet he died, but with unwonted force
Seem'd with some fancied being to discourse: 285
He knew not us, or with accustom'd art
He hid the knowledge, yet exposed his heart;
'Twas part confession and the rest defence,
A madman's tale, with gleams of waking sense.
   'I'll tell you all,' he said, 'the very day   290
When the old man first placed them in my way:
My father's spirit – he who always tried
To give me trouble, when he lived and died –
When he was gone he could not be content
To see my days in painful labour spent,   295
But would appoint his meetings, and he made
Me watch at these, and so neglect my trade.
   "'T was one hot noon, all silent, still, serene,
No living being had I lately seen;
I paddled up and down and dipp'd my net,   300
But (such his pleasure) I could nothing get, –
A father's pleasure, when his toil was done,
To plague and torture thus an only son!
And so I sat and look'd upon the stream,
How it ran on, and felt as in a dream: 305
But dream it was not: No! – I fix'd my eyes
On the mid stream and saw the spirits rise:
I saw my father on the water stand,
And hold a thin pale boy in either hand;
And there they glided ghastly on the top   310
Of the salt flood, and never touch'd a drop:
I would have struck them, but they knew th'intent,
And smiled upon the oar, and down they went.
   'Now, from that day, whenever I began
To dip my net, there stood the hard old man –   315
He and those boys: I humbled me and pray'd

They would be gone; – they heeded not, but stay'd:
Nor could I turn, nor would the boat go by,
But, gazing on the spirits, there was I:
They bade me leap to death, but I was loth to die: 320
And every day, as sure as day arose,
Would these three spirits meet me ere the close;
To hear and mark them daily was my doom,
And "Come," they said, with weak, sad voices, "come."
To row away, with all my strength I tried,   325
But there were they, hard by me in the tide,
The three unbodied forms – and "Come," still "come," they
                       cried.

   'Fathers should pity – but this old man shook
His hoary locks, and froze me by a look:
Thrice, when I struck them, through the water came   330
A hollow groan, that weaken'd all my frame:
"Father!" said I, "have mercy:" – he replied,
I know not what – the angry spirit lied, –
"Didst thou not draw thy knife?" said he: – 'T was true,
But I had pity and my arm withdrew: 335
He cried for mercy, which I kindly gave,
But he has no compassion in his grave.
   'There were three places, where they ever rose, –
The whole long river has not such as those –
Places accursed, where, if a man remain,   340
He'll see the things which strike him to the brain;
And there they made me on my paddle lean,
And look at them for hours; – accursed scene!
When they would glide to that smooth eddy-space,
Then bid me leap and join them in the place;   345
And at my groans each little villain sprite
Enjoy'd my pains and vanish'd in delight.
   'In one fierce summer-day, when my poor brain
Was burning hot, and cruel was my pain,
Then came this father-foe, and there he stood   350
With his two boys again upon the flood:
There was more mischief in their eyes, more glee,
In their pale faces when they glared at me:
Still did they force me on the oar to rest,
And when they saw me fainting and oppress'd,   355

He, with his hand, the old man, scoop'd the flood,
And there came flame about him mix'd with blood;
He bade me stoop and look upon the place,
Then flung the hot-red liquor in my face;
Burning it blazed, and then I roar'd for pain,   360
I thought the demons would have turn'd my brain.
    'Still there they stood, and forced me to behold
A place of horrors – they can not be told –
Where the flood open'd, there I heard the shriek
Of tortured guilt – no earthly tongue can speak: 365
"All days alike! for ever!" did they say,
"And unremitted torments every day" –
Yes, so they said' – But here he ceased, and gazed
On all around, affrighten'd and amazed;
And still he tried to speak, and look'd in dread   370
Of frighten'd females gathering round his bed;
Then dropp'd exhausted, and appear'd at rest,
Till the strong foe the vital powers possess'd;
Then with an inward, broken voice he cried,
'Again they come,' and mutter'd as he died.   375

Prisons

'T is well – that Man to all the varying states
Of good and ill his mind accommodates;
He not alone progressive grief sustains,
But soon submits to unexperienced pains:
Change after change, all climes his body bears;   5
His mind repeated shocks of changing cares:
Faith and fair Virtue arm the nobler breast;
Hope and mere want of feeling aid the rest.
    Or who could bear to lose the balmy air
Of summer's breath, from all things fresh and fair,   10
With all that man admires or loves below;
All earth and water, wood and vale bestow,
Where rosy pleasures smile, whence real blessings flow;

With sight and sound of every kind that lives,
And crowning all with joy that freedom gives? 15
   Who could from these, in some unhappy day,
Bear to be drawn by ruthless arms away,
To the vile nuisance of a noisome room,
Where only insolence and misery come?
(Save that the curious will by chance appear, 20
Or some in pity drop a fruitless tear;)
To a damp Prison, where the very sight
Of the warm sun is favour and not right;
Where all we hear or see the feelings shock,
The oath and groan, the fetter and the lock? 25
   Who could bear this and live? – Oh! many a year
All this is borne, and miseries more severe;
And some there are, familiar with the scene,
Who live in mirth, though few become serene.
   Far as I might the inward man perceive, 30
There was a constant effort – not to grieve:
Not to despair, for better days would come,
And the freed debtor smile again at home:
Subdued his habits, he may peace regain,
And bless the woes that were not sent in vain. 35
   Thus might we class the Debtors here confined,
The more deceived, the more deceitful kind;
Here are the guilty race, who mean to live
On credit, that credulity will give;
Who purchase, conscious they can never pay; 40
Who know their fate, and traffic to betray;
On whom no pity, fear, remorse, prevail,
Their aim a statute, their resource a jail; –
These as the public spoilers we regard,
No dun so harsh, no creditor so hard. 45
   A second kind are they, who truly strive
To keep their sinking credit long alive;
Success, nay prudence, they may want, but yet
They would be solvent, and deplore a debt;
All means they use, to all expedients run, 50
And are by slow, sad steps, at last undone:
Justly, perhaps, you blame their want of skill,

But mourn their feelings and absolve their will.
　　There is a Debtor, who his trifling *all*
Spreads in a shop; it would not fill a stall: 55
There at one window his temptation lays,
And in new modes disposes and displays:
Above the door you shall his name behold,
And what he vends in ample letters told,
The words 'Repository', 'Warehouse', all   60
He uses to enlarge concerns so small:
He to his goods assigns some beauty's name,
Then in her reign, and hopes they'll share her fame,
And talks of credit, commerce, traffic, trade,
As one important by their profit made;   65
But who can paint the vacancy, the gloom,
And spare dimensions of one backward room?
Wherein he dines, if so 't is fit to speak
Of one day's herring and the morrow's steak:
An anchorite in diet, all his care   70
Is to display his stock and vend his ware.
　　Long waiting hopeless, then he tries to meet
A kinder fortune in a distant street;
There he again displays, increasing yet
Corroding sorrow and consuming debt: 75
Alas! he wants the requisites to rise –
The true connections, the availing ties;
They who proceed on certainties advance,
These are not times when men prevail by chance:
But still he tries, till, after years of pain,   80
He finds, with anguish, he has tried in vain.
Debtors are these on whom 't is hard to press,
'Tis base, impolitic, and merciless.
　　To these we add a miscellaneous kind,
By pleasure, pride, and indolence confined;   85
Those whom no calls, no warnings could divert,
The unexperienced and the inexpert;
The builder, idler, schemer, gamester, sot, –
The follies different, but the same their lot;
Victims of horses, lasses, drinking, dice,   90
Of every passion, humour, whim, and vice.

See! that sad Merchant, who but yesterday
Had a vast household in command and pay;
He now entreats permission to employ
A boy he needs, and then entreats the boy.   95
　　And there sits one, improvident but kind,
Bound for a friend, whom honour could not bind;
Sighing, he speaks to any who appear,
'A treach'rous friend – 't was that which sent me here:
I was too kind, – I thought I could depend   100
On his bare word – he was a treach'rous friend.'
　　A Female too! – it is to her a home,
She came before – and she again will come:
Her friends have pity; when their anger drops,
They take her home; – she's tried her schools and shops – 105
Plan after plan; – but fortune would not mend,
She to herself was still the treach'rous friend;
And wheresoe'er began, all here was sure to end:
And there she sits, as thoughtless and as gay
As if she'd means, or not a debt to pay –   110
Or knew to-morrow she'd be call'd away –
Or felt a shilling and could dine to-day.
　　While thus observing, I began to trace
The sober'd features of a well-known face –
Looks once familiar, manners form'd to please,   115
And all illumined by a heart at ease:
But fraud and flattery ever claim'd a part
(Still unresisted) of that easy heart;
But he at length beholds me – 'Ah! my friend!
And have thy pleasures this unlucky end?'   120
　　'Too sure,' he said, and smiling as he sigh'd;
'I went astray, though Prudence seem'd my guide;
All she proposed I in my heart approved,
And she was honour'd, but my pleasure loved –
Pleasure, the mistress to whose arms I fled,   125
From wife-like lectures angry Prudence read.
　　'Why speak the madness of a life like mine,
The powers of beauty, novelty, and wine?
Why paint the wanton smile, the venal vow,
Or friends whose worth I can appreciate now;   130

Oft I perceived my fate, and then could say,
I'll think to-morrow, I must live to-day:
So am I here – I own the laws are just –
And here, where thought is painful, think I must:
But speech is pleasant: this discourse with thee   135
Brings to my mind the sweets of liberty,
Breaks on the sameness of the place, and gives
The doubtful heart conviction that it lives.
    'Let me describe my anguish in the hour
When law detain'd me and I felt its power.   140
    'When, in that shipwreck, this I found my shore,
And join'd the wretched, who were wreck'd before;
When I perceived each feature in the face,
Pinch'd through neglect or turbid by disgrace;
When in these wasting forms affliction stood   145
In my afflicted view, it chill'd my blood; –
And forth I rush'd, a quick retreat to make,
Till a loud laugh proclaim'd the dire mistake:
But when the groan had settled to a sigh,
When gloom became familiar to the eye,   150
When I perceive how others seem to rest,
With every evil rankling in my breast, –
Led by example, I put on the man,
Sing off my sighs, and trifle as I can.
    'Homer! nay Pope! (for never will I seek   155
Applause for learning – nought have I with Greek)
Gives us the secrets of his pagan hell,
Where ghost with ghost in sad communion dwell;
Where shade meets shade, and round the gloomy meads
They glide, and speak of old heroic deeds, –   160
What fields they conquer'd, and what foes they slew,
And sent to join the melancholy crew.
When a new spirit in that world was found,
A thousand shadowy forms came flitting round;
Those who had known him, fond enquiries made, –   165
"Of all we left, inform us, gentle shade,
Now as we lead thee in our realms to dwell,
Our twilight groves, and meads of asphodel."
    'What paints the poet, is our station here,

Where we like ghosts and flitting shades appear: 170
This is the hell he sings, and here we meet,
And former deeds to new-made friends repeat;
Heroic deeds, which here obtain us fame,
And are in fact the causes why we came:
Yes! this dim region is old Homer's hell,   175
Abate but groves and meads of asphodel.
Here, when a stranger from your world we spy,
We gather round him and for news apply;
He hears unheeding, nor can speech endure,
But shivering gazes on the vast obscure: 180
We smiling pity, and by kindness show
We felt his feelings and his terrors know;
Then speak of comfort – time will give him sight,
Where now 't is dark; where now 't is wo – delight.
    ' "Have hope," we say, "and soon the place to thee   185
Shall not a prison but a castle be:
When to the wretch whom care and guilt confound,
The world's a prison, with a wider bound;
Go where he may, he feels himself confined,
And wears the fetters of an abject mind."   190
    'But now adieu! those giant-keys appear,
Thou art not worthy to be inmate here:
Go to thy world, and to the young declare
What we, our spirits and employments, are;
Tell them how we the ills of life endure,   195
Our empire stable, and our state secure;
Our dress, our diet, for their use describe,
And bid them haste to join the gen'rous tribe:
Go to thy world, and leave us here to dwell,
Who to its joys and comforts bid farewell.'   200
    Farewell to these; but other scenes I view,
And other griefs, and guilt of deeper hue;
Where Conscience gives to outward ills her pain,
Gloom to the night, and pressure to the chain:
Here separate cells awhile in misery keep   205
Two doom'd to suffer: there they strive for sleep;
By day indulged, in larger space they range,
Their bondage certain, but their bounds have change.

One was a female, who had grievous ill
Wrought in revenge, and she enjoy'd it still: 210
With death before her, and her fate in view,
Unsated vengeance in her bosom grew:
Sullen she was and threat'ning; in her eye
Glared the stern triumph that she dared to die:
But first a being in the world must leave –   215
'T was once reproach; 't was now a short reprieve.
    She was a pauper bound, who early gave
Her mind to vice and doubly was a slave:
Upbraided, beaten, held by rough control,
Revenge sustain'd, inspired, and fill'd her soul: 220
She fired a full-stored barn, confess'd the fact,
And laugh'd at law and justified the act:
Our gentle Vicar tried his powers in vain,
She answer'd not, or answer'd with disdain;
Th' approaching fate she heard without a sigh,   225
And neither cared to live nor fear'd to die.
    Not so he felt, who with her was to pay
The forfeit, life – with dread he view'd the day,
And that short space which yet for him remain'd,
Till with his limbs his faculties were chain'd: 230
He paced his narrow bounds some ease to find,
But found it not, – no comfort reach'd his mind:
Each sense was palsied; when he tasted food,
He sigh'd and said, 'Enough – 't is very good.'
Since his dread sentence, nothing seem'd to be   235
As once it was – he seeing could not see,
Nor hearing, hear aright; – when first I came
Within his view, I fancied there was shame,
I judged resentment; I mistook the air, –
These fainter passions live not with despair;   240
Or but exist and die: – Hope, fear, and love,
Joy, doubt, and hate, may other spirits move,
But touch not his, who every waking hour
Has one fix'd dread, and always feels its power.
    'But will not Mercy?' – No! she cannot plead   245
For such an outrage; – 't was a cruel deed:
He stopp'd a timid traveller; – to his breast,

With oaths and curses, was the danger press'd: –
No! he must suffer; pity we may find
For one man's pangs, but must not wrong mankind.   250

    Still I behold him, every thought employ'd,
On one dire view! – all others are destroy'd;
This makes his features ghastly, gives the tone
Of his few words resemblance to a groan;
He takes his tasteless food, and when 't is done,   255
Counts up his meals, now lessen'd by that one;
For expectation is on time intent,
Whether he brings us joy or punishment.

    Yes! e'en in sleep the impressions all remain,
He hears the sentence and he feels the chain;   260
He sees the judge and jury, when he shakes,
And loudly cries, 'Not guilty,' and awakes:
Then chilling tremblings o'er his body creep,
Till worn-out nature is compell'd to sleep.

    Now comes the dream again: it shows each scene,   265
With each small circumstance that comes between –
The call to suffering and the very deed –
There crowds go with him, follow, and precede;
Some heartless shout, some pity, all condemn,
While he in fancied envy looks at them: 270
He seems the place for that sad act to see,
And dreams the very thirst which then will be:
A priest attends – it seems, the one he knew
In his best days, beneath whose care he grew.

    At this his terrors take a sudden flight,   275
He sees his native village with delight;
The house, the chamber, where he once array'd
His youthful person; where he knelt and pray'd:
Then too the comforts he enjoy'd at home,
The days of joy; the joys themselves are come; –   280
The hours of innocence; – the timid look
Of his loved maid, when first her hand he took,
And told his hope; her trembling joy appears,
Her forced reserve and his retreating fears.

    All now is present; – 'tis a moment's gleam   285
Of former sunshine – stay, delightful dream!

Let him within his pleasant garden walk,
Give him her arm, of blessings let them talk.
  Yes! all are with him now, and all the while
Life's early prospects and his Fanny's smile: 290
Then come his sister and his village-friend,
And he will now the sweetest moments spend
Life has to yield; – No! never will he find
Again on earth such pleasure in his mind:
He goes through shrubby walks these friends among,   295
Love in their looks and honour on the tongue:
Nay, there's a charm beyond what nature shows,
The bloom is softer and more sweetly glows; –
Pierced by no crime, and urged by no desire
For more than true and honest hearts require,   300
They feel the calm delight, and thus proceed
Through the green lane, – then linger in the mead, –
Stray o'er the heath in all its purple bloom, –
And pluck the blossom where the wild bees hum;
Then through the broomy bound with ease they pass,   305
And press the sandy sheep-walk's slender grass,
Where dwarfish flowers among the gorse are spread,
And the lamb browses by the linnet's bed;
Then 'cross the bounding brook they make their way
O'er its rough bridge – and there behold the bay! –   310
The ocean smiling to the fervid sun –
The waves that faintly fall and slowly run –
The ships at distance and the boats at hand;
And now they walk upon the sea-side sand,
Counting the number and what kind they be,   315
Ships softly sinking in the sleepy sea:
Now arm in arm, now parted, they behold
The glitt'ring waters on the shingles roll'd:
The timid girls, half dreading their design,
Dip the small foot in the retarded brine,   320
And search for crimson weeds, which spreading flow,
Or lie like pictures on the sand below:
With all those bright red pebbles, that the sun
Through the small waves so softly shines upon;
And those live lucid jellies which the eye   325

Delights to trace as they swim glittering by:
Pearl-shells and rubied star-fish they admire,
And will arrange above the parlour-fire, –
Tokens of bliss! – 'Oh! horrible! a wave
Roars as it rises – save me, Edward! save!'   330
She cries: – Alas! the watchman on his way
Calls, and lets in – truth, terror, and the day!

The Frank Courtship

Grave Jonas Kindred, Sybil Kindred's sire,
Was six feet high, and look'd six inches higher;
Erect, morose, determined, solemn, slow,
Who knew the man, could never cease to know;
His faithful spouse, when Jonas was not by,   5
Had a firm presence and a steady eye;
But with her husband dropp'd her look and tone,
And Jonas ruled unquestion'd and alone.
    He read, and oft would quote the sacred words,
How pious husbands of their wives were lords;   10
Sarah call'd Abraham Lord! and who could be,
So Jonas thought, a greater man than he?
Himself he view'd with undisguised respect,
And never pardon'd freedom or neglect.
    They had one daughter, and this favourite child   15
Had oft the father of his spleen beguiled;
Soothed by attention from her early years,
She gain'd all wishes by her smiles or tears:
But Sybil then was in that playful time,
When contradiction is not held a crime;   20
When parents yield their children idle praise
For faults corrected in their after days.
    Peace in the sober house of Jonas dwelt,
Where each his duty and his station felt:
Yet not that peace some favour'd mortals find,   25
In equal views and harmony of mind;

Not the soft peace that blesses those who love,
Where all with one consent in union move;
But it was that which one superior will
Commands, by making all inferiors still;   30
Who bids all murmurs, all objections cease,
And with imperious voice announces – Peace!
    They were, to wit, a remnant of that crew,
Who, as their foes maintain, their Sovereign slew;
An independent race, precise, correct,   35
Who ever married in the kindred sect:
No son or daughter of their order wed
A friend to England's king who lost his head;
Cromwell was still their Saint, and when they met,
They mourn'd that Saints were not our rulers yet.   40
    Fix'd were their habits; they arose betimes,
Then pray'd their hour, and sang their party-rhymes:
Their meals were plenteous, regular and plain;
The trade of Jonas brought him constant gain;
Vender of hops and malt, of coals and corn –   45
And, like his father, he was merchant born:
Neat was their house; each table, chair, and stool,
Stood in its place, or moving moved by rule;
No lively print or picture graced the room;
A plain brown paper lent its decent gloom;   50
But here the eye, in glancing round, survey'd
A small recess that seem'd for china made;
Such pleasing pictures seem'd this pencill'd ware,
That few would search for nobler objects there –
Yet, turn'd by chosen friends, and there appear'd   55
His stern, strong features, whom they all revered;
For there in lofty air was seen to stand
The bold Protector of the conquer'd land;
Drawn in that look with which he wept and swore,
Turn'd out the Members, and made fast the door,   60
Ridding the House of every knave and drone,
Forced, though it grieved his soul, to rule alone.
The stern still smile each friend approving gave,
Then turn'd the view, and all again were grave.
    There stood a clock, though small the owner's need,   65
For habit told when all things should proceed;

Few their amusements, but when friends appear'd,
They with the world's distress their spirits cheer'd;
The nation's guilt, that would not long endure
The reign of men so modest and so pure: 70
Their town was large, and seldom pass'd a day
But some had fail'd, and others gone astray;
Clerks had absconded, wives eloped, girls flown
To Gretna-Green, or sons rebellious grown;
Quarrels and fires arose; – and it was plain   75
The times were bad; the Saints had ceased to reign!
A few yet lived, to languish and to mourn
For good old manners never to return.
     Jonas had sisters, and of these was one
Who lost a husband and an only son: 80
Twelve months her sables she in sorrow wore,
And mourn'd so long that she could mourn no more.
Distant from Jonas, and from all her race,
She now resided in a lively place;
There, by the sect unseen, at whist she play'd,   85
Nor was of churchmen or their church afraid:
If much of this the graver brother heard,
He something censured, but he little fear'd;
He knew her rich and frugal; for the rest,
He felt no care, or, if he felt, suppress'd: 90
Nor for companion when she ask'd her Niece,
Had he suspicions that disturb'd his peace;
Frugal and rich, these virtues as a charm
Preserved the thoughtful man from all alarm;
An infant yet, she soon would home return,   95
Nor stay the manners of the world to learn;
Meantime his boys would all his care engross,
And be his comforts if he felt the loss.
     The sprightly Sybil, pleased and unconfined,
Felt the pure pressure of the op'ning mind: 100
All here was gay and cheerful – all at home
Unvaried quiet and unruffled gloom:
There were no changes, and amusements few; –
Here, all was varied, wonderful, and new;
There were plain meals, plain dresses, and grave looks –   105
Here, gay companions and amusing books;

And the young Beauty soon began to taste
The light vocations of the scene she graced.
   A man of business feels it as a crime
On calls domestic to consume his time;   110
Yet this grave man had not so cold a heart,
But with his daughter he was grieved to part:
And he demanded that in every year
The Aunt and Niece should at his house appear.
   'Yes! we must go, my child, and by our dress   115
A grave conformity of mind express;
Must sing at meeting, and from cards refrain,
The more t' enjoy when we return again.'
   Thus spake the Aunt, and the discerning child
Was pleased to learn how fathers are beguiled.   120
Her artful part the young dissembler took,
And from the matron caught th' approving look:
When thrice the friends had met, excuse was sent
For more delay, and Jonas was content;
Till a tall maiden by her sire was seen,   125
In all the bloom and beauty of sixteen;
He gazed admiring: – she, with visage prim,
Glanced an arch look of gravity on him;
For she was gay at heart, but wore disguise,
And stood a vestal in her father's eyes;   130
Pure, pensive, simple, sad; the damsel's heart,
When Jonas praised, reproved her for the part;
For Sybil, fond of pleasure, gay and light,
Had still a secret bias to the right;
Vain as she was – and flattery made her vain –   135
Her simulation gave her bosom pain.
   Again return'd, the Matron and the Niece
Found the late quiet gave their joy increase;
The aunt infirm, no more her visits paid,
But still with her sojourn'd the favourite maid.   140
Letters were sent when franks could be procured,
And when they could not, silence was endured;
All were in health, and if they older grew,
It seem'd a fact that none among them knew;
The aunt and niece still led a pleasant life,   145
And quiet days had Jonas and his wife.

Near him a Widow dwelt of worthy fame,
Like his her manners, and her creed the same;
The wealth her husband left, her care retain'd
For one tall Youth, and widow she remain'd;   150
His love respectful all her care repaid,
Her wishes watch'd, and her commands obey'd.
   Sober he was and grave from early youth,
Mindful of forms, but more intent on truth;
In a light drab he uniformly dress'd,   155
And look serene th' unruffled mind express'd;
A hat with ample verge his brows o'erspread,
And his brown locks curl'd graceful on his head;
Yet might observers in his speaking eye
Some observation, some acuteness spy;   160
The friendly thought it keen, the treacherous deem'd it sly;
Yet not a crime could foe or friend detect,
His actions all were, like his speech, correct;
And they who jested on a mind so sound,
Upon his virtues must their laughter found;   165
Chaste, sober, solemn, and devout they named
Him who was thus, and not of *this* ashamed.
   Such were the virtues Jonas found in one
In whom he warmly wish'd to find a son:
Three years had pass'd since he had Sybil seen;   170
But she was doubtless what she once had been,
Lovely and mild, obedient and discreet;
The pair must love whenever they should meet;
Then ere the widow or her son should choose
Some happier maid, he would explain his views: 175
Now she, like him, was politic and shrewd,
With strong desire of lawful gain embued;
To all he said, she bow'd with much respect,
Pleased to comply, yet seeming to reject;
Cool and yet eager, each admired the strength   180
Of the opponent, and agreed at length:
As a drawn battle shows to each a force,
Powerful as his, he honours it of course;
So in these neighbours, each the power discern'd,
And gave the praise that was to each return'd.   185
   Jonas now ask'd his daughter – and the Aunt,

Though loth to lose her, was obliged to grant: –
But would not Sybil to the matron cling,
And fear to leave the shelter of her wing?
No! in the young there lives a love of change,   190
And to the easy, they prefer the strange!
Then, too, the joys she once pursued with zeal,
From whist and visits sprung, she ceased to feel:
When with the matrons Sybil first sat down,
To cut for partners and to stake her crown,   195
This to the youthful maid preferment seem'd,
Who thought what woman she was then esteem'd;
But in few years, when she perceived, indeed,
The real woman to the girl succeed,
No longer tricks and honours fill'd her mind,   200
But other feelings, not so well defined;
She then reluctant grew, and thought it hard,
To sit and ponder o'er an ugly card;
Rather the nut-tree shade the nymph preferr'd,
Pleased with the pensive gloom and evening bird;   205
Thither, from company retired, she took
The silent walk, or read the fav'rite book.
    The father's letter, sudden, short, and kind,
Awaked her wonder, and disturb'd her mind;
She found new dreams upon her fancy seize,   210
Wild roving thoughts and endless reveries:
The parting came; – and when the Aunt perceived
The tears of Sybil, and how much she grieved –
To love for her that tender grief she laid,
That various, soft, contending passions made.   215
    When Sybil rested in her father's arms,
His pride exulted in a daughter's charms;
A maid accomplish'd he was pleased to find,
Nor seem'd the form more lovely than the mind:
But when the fit of pride and fondness fled,   220
He saw his judgment by his hopes misled;
High were the lady's spirits, far more free
Her mode of speaking than a maid's should be;
Too much, as Jonas thought, she seem'd to know,
And all her knowledge was disposed to show;   225
'Too gay her dress, like theirs who idly dote

On a young coxcomb, or a coxcomb's coat;
In foolish spirits when our friends appear,
And vainly grave when not a man is near.'
   Thus Jonas, adding to his sorrow blame,   230
And terms disdainful to a Sister's name: –
'The sinful wretch has by her arts defiled
The ductile spirit of my darling child.'
   'The maid is virtuous,' said the dame – Quoth he
'Let her give proof, by acting virtuously: 235
Is it in gaping when the Elders pray?
In reading nonsense half a summer's day?
In those mock forms that she delights to trace,
Or her loud laughs in Hezekiah's face?
She – O Susanna! – to the world belongs;   240
She loves the follies of its idle throngs,
And reads soft tales of love, and sings love's soft'ning songs.
But, as our friend is yet delay'd in town,
We must prepare her till the Youth comes down:
You shall advise the maiden; I will threat;   245
Her fears and hopes may yield us comfort yet.'
   Now the grave father took the lass aside,
Demanding sternly, 'Wilt thou be a bride?'
She answer'd, calling up an air sedate,
'I have not vow'd against the holy state.'   250
   'No folly, Sybil,' said the parent; 'know
What to their parents virtuous maidens owe:
A worthy, wealthy youth, whom I approve,
Must thou prepare to honour and to love.
Formal to thee his air and dress may seem,   255
But the good youth is worthy of esteem:
Shouldst thou with rudeness treat him; of disdain
Should he with justice or of slight complain,
Or of one taunting speech give certain proof,
Girl! I reject thee from my sober roof.'   260
   'My aunt,' said Sybil, 'will with pride protect
One whom a father can for this reject;
Nor shall a formal, rigid, soul-less boy
My manners alter, or my views destroy!'
   Jonas then lifted up his hands on high,   265
And, utt'ring something 'twixt a groan and sigh,

Left the determined maid, her doubtful mother by.
　'Hear me,' she said; 'incline thy heart, my child,
And fix thy fancy on a man so mild:
Thy father, Sybil, never could be moved   270
By one who loved him, or by one he loved.
Union like ours is but a bargain made
By slave and tyrant – he will be obey'd;
Then calls the quiet, comfort – but thy Youth
Is mild by nature, and as frank as truth.'   275
　'But will he love?' said Sybil; 'I am told
That these mild creatures are by nature cold.'
　'Alas!' the matron answer'd, 'much I dread
That dangerous love by which the young are led!
That love is earthy; you the creature prize,   280
And trust your feelings and believe your eyes:
Can eyes and feelings inward worth descry?
No! my fair daughter, on our choice rely!
Your love, like that display'd upon the stage,
Indulged is folly, and opposed is rage; –   285
More prudent love our sober couples show,
All that to mortal beings, mortals owe;
All flesh is grass – before you give a heart,
Remember, Sybil, that in death you part;
And should your husband die before your love,   290
What needless anguish must a widow prove!
No! my fair child, let all such visions cease;
Yield but esteem, and only try for peace.'
　'I must be loved,' said Sybil; 'I must see
The man in terrors who aspires to me;   295
At my forbidding frown his heart must ache,
His tongue must falter, and his frame must shake:
And if I grant him at my feet to kneel,
What trembling, fearful pleasure must he feel;
Nay, such the raptures that my smiles inspire,   300
That reason's self must for a time retire.'
　'Alas! for good Josiah,' said the dame,
'These wicked thoughts would fill his soul with shame;
He kneel and tremble at a thing of dust!
He cannot, child:' – the Child replied, 'He must.'   305
　They ceased: the matron left her with a frown;

So Jonas met her when the Youth came down:
'Behold,' said he, 'thy future spouse attends;
Receive him, daughter, as the best of friends;
Observe, respect him – humble be each word,   310
That welcomes home thy husband and thy lord.'
    Forewarn'd, thought Sybil, with a bitter smile,
I shall prepare my manner and my style.
    Ere yet Josiah enter'd on his task,
The father met him – 'Deign to wear a mask   315
A few dull days, Josiah, – but a few –
It is our duty, and the sex's due;
I wore it once, and every grateful wife
Repays it with obedience through her life:
Have no regard to Sybil's dress, have none   320
To her pert language, to her flippant tone;
Henceforward thou shalt rule unquestion'd and alone;
And she thy pleasure in thy looks shall seek –
How she shall dress, and whether she may speak.'
    A sober smile return'd the Youth, and said,   325
'Can I cause fear, who am myself afraid?'
    Sybil, meantime, sat thoughtful in her room,
And often wonder'd – 'Will the creature come?
Nothing shall tempt, shall force me to bestow
My hand upon him, – yet I wish to know.'   330
    The door unclosed, and she beheld her sire
Lead in the Youth, then hasten to retire;
'Daughter, my friend – my daughter, friend' – he cried,
And gave a meaning look, and stepp'd aside;
That look contain'd a mingled threat and prayer,   335
'Do take him, child – offend him, if you dare.'
    The couple gazed – were silent, and the maid
Look'd in his face, to make the man afraid;
The man, unmoved, upon the maiden cast
A steady view – so salutation pass'd: 340
But in this instant Sybil's eye had seen
The tall fair person, and the still staid mien;
The glow that temp'rance o'er the cheek had spread,
Where the soft down half veil'd the purest red;
And the serene deportment that proclaim'd   345
A heart unspotted, and a life unblamed:

But then with these she saw attire too plain,
The pale brown coat, though worn without a stain;
The formal air, and something of the pride
That indicates the wealth it seems to hide;   350
And looks that were not, she conceived, exempt
From a proud pity, or a sly contempt.
    Josiah's eyes had their employment too,
Engaged and soften'd by so bright a view;
A fair and meaning face, an eye of fire,   355
That check'd the bold, and made the free retire:
But then with these he mark'd the studied dress
And lofty air, that scorn or pride express;
With that insidious look, that seem'd to hide
In an affected smile the scorn and pride;   360
And if his mind the virgin's meaning caught,
He saw a foe with treacherous purpose fraught –
Captive the heart to take, and to reject it, caught.
    Silent they sate – thought Sybil, that he seeks
Something, no doubt; I wonder if he speaks: 365
Scarcely she wonder'd, when these accents fell
Slow in her ear – 'Fair maiden, art thou well?'
'Art thou physician?' she replied; 'my hand,
My pulse, at least, shall be at thy command.'
    She said – and saw, surprised, Josiah kneel,   370
And gave his lips the offer'd pulse to feel;
The rosy colour rising in her cheek,
Seem'd that surprise unmix'd with wrath to speak;
Then sternness she assumed, and – 'Doctor, tell,
Thy words cannot alarm me – am I well?'   375
    'Thou art,' said he; 'and yet thy dress so light,
I do conceive, some danger must excite.'
'In whom?' said Sybil, with a look demure:
'In more,' said he, 'than I expect to cure; –
I, in thy light luxuriant robe, behold   380
Want and excess, abounding and yet cold;
Here needed, there display'd, in many a wanton fold:
Both health and beauty, learned authors show,
From a just medium in our clothing flow.'
    'Proceed, good doctor; if so great my need,   385
What is thy fee? Good doctor! pray proceed.'

'Large is my fee, fair lady, but I take
None till some progress in my cure I make:
Thou hast disease, fair maiden; thou art vain;
Within that face sit insult and disdain;   390
Thou art enamour'd of thyself; my art
Can see the naughty malice of thy heart:
With a strong pleasure would thy bosom move,
Were I to own thy power, and ask thy love;
And such thy beauty, damsel, that I might,   395
But for thy pride, feel danger in thy sight,
And lose my present peace in dreams of vain delight.'
    'And can thy patients,' said the nymph, 'endure
Physic like this? and will it work a cure?'
    'Such is my hope, fair damsel; thou, I find,   400
Hast the true tokens of a noble mind;
But the world wins thee, Sybil, and thy joys
Are placed in trifles, fashions, follies, toys;
Thou hast sought pleasure in the world around,
That in thine own pure bosom should be found: 405
Did all that world admire thee, praise and love,
Could it the least of nature's pains remove?
Could it for errors, follies, sins atone,
Or give thee comfort, thoughtful and alone?
It has, believe me, maid, no power to charm   410
Thy soul from sorrow, or thy flesh from harm:
Turn then, fair creature, from a world of sin,
And seek the jewel happiness within.'
    'Speak'st thou at meeting?' said the nymph; 'thy speech
Is that of mortal very prone to teach;   415
But wouldst thou, doctor, from the patient learn
Thine own disease? – The cure is thy concern.'
'Yea, with good will.' – 'Then know 'tis thy complaint,
That, for a sinner, thou 'rt too much a saint;
Hast too much show of the sedate and pure,   420
And without cause art formal and demure:
This makes a man unsocial, unpolite;
Odious when wrong, and insolent if right.
Thou may'st be good, but why should goodness be
Wrapt in a garb of such formality?   425
Thy person well might please a damsel's eye,

In decent habit with a scarlet dye;
But, jest apart – what virtue canst thou trace
In that broad brim that hides thy sober face?
Does that long-skirted drab, that over-nice   430
And formal clothing, prove a scorn of vice?
Then for thine accent – what in sound can be
So void of grace as dull monotony?
Love has a thousand varied notes to move
The human heart: – thou may'st not speak of love,   435
Till thou hast cast thy formal ways aside,
And those becoming youth and nature tried:
Not till exterior freedom, spirit, ease,
Prove it thy study and delight to please;
Not till these follies meet thy just disdain,   440
While yet thy virtues and thy worth remain.'
   'This is severe! – Oh! maiden, wilt not thou
Something for habits, manners, modes, allow?' –
'Yes! but allowing much, I much require,
In my behalf, for manners, modes, attire!'   445
   'True, lovely Sybil; and, this point agreed,
Let me to those of greater weight proceed:
Thy father!' – 'Nay,' she quickly interposed,
'Good doctor, here our conference is closed!'
   Then left the Youth, who, lost in his retreat,   450
Pass'd the good matron on her garden-seat;
His looks were troubled , and his air, once mild
And calm, was hurried: – 'My audacious child!'
Exclaim'd the dame, 'I read what she has done
In thy displeasure – Ah! the thoughtless one: 455
But yet, Josiah, to my stern good man
Speak of the maid as mildly as you can:
Can you not seem to woo a little while
The daughter's will, the father to beguile?
So that his wrath in time may wear away;   460
Will you preserve our peace, Josiah? say.'
   'Yes! my good neighbour,' said the gentle youth,
'Rely securely on my care and truth;
And should thy comfort with my efforts cease;

And only then, – perpetual is thy peace.'   465
The dame had doubts: she well his virtues knew,
His deeds were friendly, and his words were true;
'But to address this vixen is a task
He is ashamed to take, and I to ask.'
Soon as the father from Josiah learn'd   470
What pass'd with Sybil, he the truth discern'd.
'He loves,' the man exclaim'd, 'he loves, 't is plain,
The thoughtless girl, and shall he love in vain?
She may be stubborn, but she shall be tried,
Born as she is of wilfulness and pride.'   475
   With anger fraught, but willing to persuade,
The wrathful father met the smiling maid:
'Sybil,' said he, 'I long, and yet I dread
To know thy conduct – hath Josiah fled?
And, grieved and fretted by thy scornful air,   480
For his lost peace, betaken him to prayer?
Couldst thou his pure and modest mind distress,
By vile remarks upon his speech, address,
Attire, and voice?' – 'All this I must confess.' –
'Unhappy child! what labour will it cost   485
To win him back!' – 'I do not think him lost.' –
'Courts he then, (trifler!) insult and disdain?' –
'No: but from these he courts me to refrain?' –
'Then hear me, Sybil – should Josiah leave
Thy father's house?' – 'My father's child would grieve:'   490
'That is of grace, and if he come again
To speak of love?' – 'I might from grief refrain.' –
'Then wilt thou, daughter, our design embrace?' –
'Can I resist it, if it be of grace?' –
'Dear child! in three plain words thy mind express –   495
Wilt thou have this good youth?' – 'Dear father! yes.'

The Magnet

Why force the backward heart on love,
    That of itself the flame might feel?
When you the Magnet's power would prove,
    Say, would you strike it on the Steel?

From common flints you may by force   5
    Excite some transient sparks of fire;
And so, in natures rude and coarse,
    Compulsion may provoke desire.

But when, approaching by degrees,
    The Magnet to the Steel draws nigh,   10
At once they feel, each other seize,
    And rest in mutual sympathy.

So must the Lover find his way
    To move the heart he hopes to win –
Must not in distant forms delay –   15
    Must not in rude assaults begin.

For such attractive power has Love,
    We justly each extreme may fear:
'Tis lost when we too distant prove,
    And when we rashly press too near.   20

Satire

I love not the satiric Muse:
No man on earth would I abuse;
Nor with empoison'd verses grieve
The most offending son of Eve.
Leave him to law, if he have done   5

What injures any other son:
It hardens man to see his name
Exposed to public mirth or shame;
And rouses, as it spoils his rest,
The baser passions of his breast.   10

    Attack a book – attack a song –
You will not do essential wrong;
You may their blemishes expose,
And yet not be the writer's foes.
But when the man you thus attack,   15
    And him expose with critic art,
You put a creature to the rack –
   You wring, you agonise, his heart.
No farther honest Satire can
    In all her enmity proceed,   20
Than passing by the wicked Man,
    To execrate the wicked Deed.

If so much virtue yet remain
That he would feel the sting and pain,
That virtue is a reason why   25
The Muse her sting should not apply:
If no such Virtue yet survive,
    What is your angry Satire worth,
But to arouse the sleeping hive,
    And send the raging Passions forth,   30
In bold, vindictive, angry flight,
To sting wherever they alight?

Smugglers and Poachers

There was a Widow in the village known
To our good Squire, and he had favour shown
By frequent bounty. – She as usual came,
And Richard saw the worn and weary frame,

Pale cheek, and eye subdued, of her whose mind   5
Was grateful still, and glad a friend to find,
Though to the world long since and all its hopes resign'd:
Her easy form, in rustic neatness clad,
Was pleasing still! but she for ever sad.
   'Deep is her grief!' said Richard, – 'truly deep,   10
And very still, and therefore seems to sleep;
To borrow simile, to paint her woes,
Theirs, like the river's motion, seems repose,
Making no petty murmuring, – settled slow,
They never waste, they never overflow.   15
Rachel is one of those – for there are some
Who look for nothing in their days to come,
No good nor evil, neither hope nor fear,
Nothing remains or cheerful or severe;
One day is like the past, the year's sweet prime   20
Like the sad fall, – for Rachel heeds not time:
Nothing remains to agitate her breast,
Spent is the tempest, and the sky at rest;
But while it raged her peace its ruin met,
And now the sun is on her prospects set; –   25
Leave her, and let us her distress explore,
She heeds it not – she has been left before.'

————

   There were two lads call'd Shelley hither brought,
But whence we know not – it was never sought;
Their wandering mother left them, left her name,   30
And the boys throve and valiant men became:
Handsome, of more than common size, and tall,
And no one's kindred, seem'd beloved of all;
All seem'd alliance by their deeds to prove,
And loved the youths who could not claim their love.   35
One was call'd James, the more sedate and grave,
The other Robert – names their neighbours gave;
They both were brave, but Robert loved to run
And meet his danger – James would rather shun
The dangerous trial, but whenever tried   40
He all his spirit to the act applied.

Robert would aid on any man bestow,
James would his man and the occasion know;
For that was quick and prompt – this temperate and slow.
Robert would all things he desired pursue,   45
James would consider what was best to do;
All spoke of Robert as a man they loved,
And most of James as valued and approved.
    Both had some learning: Robert his acquired
By quicker parts, and was by praise inspired;   50
James, as he was in his acquirements slow,
Would learn the worth of what he tried to know.
In fact, this youth was generous – that was just;
The one you loved, the other you would trust:
Yet him you loved you would for truth approve,   55
And him you trusted you would likewise love.
    Such were the brothers – James had found his way
To Nether Hall, and there inclined to stay;
He could himself command, and therefore could obey:
He with the keeper took his daily round,   60
A rival grew, and some unkindness found;
But his superior farm'd! the place was void,
And James guns, dogs, and dignity enjoy'd.
    Robert had scorn of service: he would be
A slave to no man – happy were the free,   65
And only they; – by such opinions led,
Robert to sundry kinds of trade was bred;
Nor let us wonder if he sometimes made
An active partner in a lawless trade;
Fond of adventure, wanton as the wave,   70
He loved the danger and the law to brave;
But these were chance-adventures, known to few, –
Not that the hero cared what people knew.
    The brothers met not often – When they met
James talk'd of honest gains and scorn of debt,   75
Of virtuous labour, of a sober life,
And what with credit would support a wife.
    But Robert answer'd, – 'How can men advise
Who to a master let their tongue and eyes?
Whose words are not their own? whose foot and hand   80
Run at a nod, or act upon command?

Who cannot eat or drink, discourse or play,
Without requesting others that they may?
    'Debt you would shun; but what advice to give
Who owe your service every hour you live!   85
Let a bell sound, and from your friends you run,
Although the darling of your heart were one;
But if the bondage fits you, I resign
You to your lot – I am content with mine!'
    Thus would the Lads their sentiments express,   90
And part in earnest, part in playfulness;
Till Love, controller of all hearts and eyes,
Breaker of bonds, of friendship's holy ties,
Awakener of new wills and slumbering sympathies,
Began his reign, – till Rachel, meek-eyed maid,   95
That form, those cheeks, that faultless face display'd,
That child of gracious nature, ever neat
And never fine; a flow'ret simply sweet,
Seeming at least unconscious she was fair;
Meek in her spirit, timid in her air,   100
And shrinking from his glance if one presumed
To come too near the beauty as it bloom'd.
    Robert beheld her in her father's cot
Day after day, and bless'd his happy lot;
He look'd indeed, but he could not offend   105
By gentle looks – he was her father's friend:
She was accustom'd to that tender look,
And frankly gave the hand he fondly took;
She loved his stories, pleased she heard him play,
Pensive herself, she loved to see him gay,   110
And if they loved not yet, they were in Love's highway.
    But Rachel now to womanhood was grown,
And would no more her faith and fondness own;
She call'd her latent prudence to her aid,
And grew observant, cautious, and afraid;   115
She heard relations of her lover's guile,
And could believe the danger of his smile:
With art insidious rival damsels strove
To show how false his speech, how feign'd his love;
And though her heart another story told,   120
Her speech grew cautious, and her manner cold.

Rachel had village fame, was fair and tall,
And gain'd a place of credit at the Hall;
Where James beheld her seated in that place,
With a child's meekness, and an angel's face;   125
Her temper soft, her spirit firm, her words
Simple and few as simple truth affords.
    James could but love her, – he at church had seen
The tall, fair maid, had met her on the green,
Admiring always, nor surprised to find   130
Her figure often present to his mind;
But now he saw her daily, and the sight
Gave him new pleasure and increased delight.
    But James, still prudent and reserved, though sure
The love he felt was love that would endure,   135
Would wait awhile, observing what was fit,
And meet, and right, nor would himself commit:
Then was he flatter'd, – James in time became
Rich, both as slayer of the Baron's game,
And as protector, – not a female dwelt   140
In that demesne who had not feign'd or felt
Regard for James; and he from all had praise
Enough a young man's vanity to raise;
With all these pleasures he of course must part,
When Rachel reign'd sole empress of his heart.   145
    Robert was now deprived of that delight
He once experienced in his mistress' sight;
For, though he now his frequent visits paid,
He saw but little of the cautious maid:
The simple common pleasures that he took   150
Grew dull, and he the wonted haunts forsook;
His flute and song he left, his book and pen,
And sought the meetings of adventurous men;
There was a love-born sadness in his breast,
That wanted stimulus to bring on rest;   155
These simple pleasures were no more of use,
And danger only could repose produce;
He join'd th' associates in their lawless trade,
And was at length of their profession made.
    He saw connected with th' adventurous crew   160
Those whom he judged were sober men and true;

He found that some, who should the trade prevent,
Gave it by purchase their encouragement;
He found that contracts could be made with those
Who had their pay these dealers to oppose;   165
And the good ladies whom at church he saw
With looks devout, of reverence and awe,
Could change their feelings as they change their place,
And, whispering, deal for spicery and lace:
And thus the craft and avarice of these   170
Urged on the youth, and gave his conscience ease.
    Him loved the maiden Rachel, fondly loved,
As many a sigh and tear in absence proved,
And many a fear for dangers that she knew,
And many a doubt what one so gay might do: 175
Of guilt she thought not, – she had often heard
They bought and sold, and nothing wrong appear'd;
Her father's maxim this: she understood
There was some ill, – but he, she knew, was good:
It was a traffic – but was done by night –   180
If wrong, how trade? why secrecy, if right?
But Robert's conscience, she believed, was pure –
And that he read his Bible she was sure.
    James, better taught, in confidence declared
His grief for what his guilty brother dared: 185
He sigh'd to think how near he was akin
To one reduced by godless men to sin;
Who, being always of the law in dread,
To other crimes were by the danger led –
And crimes with like excuse. – The Smuggler cries,   190
'What guilt is his who pays for what he buys?'
The Poacher questions, with perverted mind,
'Were not the gifts of Heaven for all design'd?'
This cries, 'I sin not – take not till I pay' –
That, 'my own hand brought down my proper prey:' –   195
And while to such fond arguments they cling,
How fear they God? how honour they the king?
Such men associate, and each other aid,
Till all are guilty, rash, and desperate made;
Till to some lawless deed the wretches fly,   200
And in the act, or for the acting, die.

The maid was frighten'd, – but, if this was true,
Robert for certain no such danger knew;
He always pray'd ere he a trip began,
And was too happy for a wicked man: 205
How could a creature, who was always gay,
So kind to all men, so disposed to pray,
How could he give his heart to such an evil way?
Yet she had fears, – for she could not believe
That James could lie, or purpose to deceive;   210
But still she found, though not without respect
For one so good, she must the man reject;
For, simple though she was, full well she knew
What this strong friendship led him to pursue;
And, let the man be honest as the light,   215
Love warps the mind a little from the right;
And she proposed, against the trying day,
What in the trial she should think and say.
    And now, their love avow'd, in both arose
Fear and disdain – the orphan pair were foes.   220
    Robert, more generous of the two, avow'd
His scorn, defiance, and contempt aloud.
    James talk'd of pity in a softer tone,
To Rachel speaking, and with her alone:
He knew full well, he said, to what must come   225
His wretched brother, what would be his doom:
Thus he her bosom fenced with dread about;
But love he could not with his skill drive out.
Still he affected something, – and that skill
Made the love wretched, though it could not kill;   230
And Robert fail'd, though much he tried, to prove
He had no guilt – She granted he had love.
    Thus they proceeded, till a winter came,
When the stern keeper told of stolen game:
Throughout the woods the poaching dogs had been,   235
And from him nothing should the robbers screen,
From him and law, – he would all hazards run,
Nor spare a poacher, were his brother one, –
Love, favour, interest, tie of blood should fail,
Till vengeance bore him bleeding to the jail.   240
    Poor Rachel shudder'd, – smuggling she could name

Without confusion, for she felt not shame;
But poachers were her terror, and a wood
Which they frequented had been mark'd by blood;
And though she thought her Robert was secure   245
In better thoughts, yet could she not be sure.
　　James now was urgent, – it would break his heart
With hope, with her, and with such views to part,
When one so wicked would her hand possess,
And he a brother! – that was his distress,   250
And must be hers, – She heard him, and she sigh'd,
Looking in doubt, – but nothing she replied.
There was a generous feeling in her mind,
That told her this was neither good nor kind:
James caused her terror, but he did no more –   255
Her love was now as it had been before.
　　Their traffic fail'd, – and the adventurous crew
No more their profitless attempts renew:
Dig they will not, and beg they might in vain –
Had they not pride, and what can then remain?   260
　· Now was the game destroy'd, and not a hare
Escaped at least the danger of the snare;
Woods of their feather'd beauty were bereft,
The beauteous victims of the silent theft;
The well-known shops received a large supply,   265
That they who could not kill at least might buy.
　　James was enraged, enraged his lord, and both
Confirm'd their threatening with a vengeful oath:
Fresh aid was sought, – and nightly on the lands
Walk'd on their watch the strong, determined bands: 270
Pardon was offer'd, and a promised pay
To him who would the desperate gang betray.
Nor fail'd the measure, – on a certain night
A few were seized – the rest escaped by flight;
Yet they resisted boldly ere they fled,   275
And blows were dealt around, and blood was shed;
Two groaning helpers on the earth were laid,
When more arrived the lawful cause to aid:
Then four determined men were seized and bound,
And Robert in this desperate number found: 280
In prison fetter'd, he deplored his fate,

And cursed the folly he perceived too late.
    James was a favourite with his lord, – the zeal
He show'd was such as masters ever feel:
If he for vengeance on a culprit cried, 285
Or if for mercy, still his lord complied;
And now, 't was said, he will for mercy plead,
For his own brother's was the guilty deed:
True, the hurt man is in a mending way,
But must be crippled to his dying day. 290
    Now James had vow'd the law should take its course,
He would not stay it, if he did not force;
He could his witness, if he pleased, withdraw,
Or he could arm with certain death the law:
This he attested to the maid, and true, 295
If this he could not, yet he much could do.
    How suffer'd then that maid, – no thought she had,
No view of days to come, that was not sad;
As sad as life with all its hopes resign'd,
As sad as aught but guilt can make mankind. 300
    With bitter grief the pleasures she review'd
Of early hope, with innocence pursued,
When she began to love, and he was fond and good:
He now must die, she heard from every tongue –
Die, and so thoughtless! perish, and so young! 305
Brave, kind, and generous, tender, constant, true,
And he must die – then will I perish too!
    A thousand acts in every age will prove
Women are valiant in a cause they love;
If fate the favour'd swain in danger place, 310
They heed not danger – perils they embrace;
They dare the world's contempt, they brave their
                      name's disgrace;
They on the ocean meet its wild alarms,
They search the dungeon with extended arms;
The utmost trial of their faith they prove, 315
And yield the lover to assert their love.
    James knew his power – his feelings were not nice –
Mercy he sold, and she must pay the price:
If his good lord forbore to urge their fate,
And he the utmost of their guilt to state, 320

The felons might their forfeit lives redeem,
And in their country's cause regain esteem;
But never more that man, whom he had shame
To call his brother, must she see or name.
    Rachel was meek, but she had firmness too,   325
And reason'd much on what she ought to do:
In Robert's place, she knew what she should choose –
But life was not the thing she fear'd to lose:
She knew that she could not their contract break,
Nor for her life a new engagement make;   330
But he was man, and guilty, – death so near
Might not to his as to her mind appear;
And he might wish, to spare that forfeit life,
The maid he loved might be his brother's wife,
Although that brother was his bitter foe,   335
And he must all the sweets of life forego.
    This would she try, – intent on this alone,
She could assume a calm and settled tone:
She spake with firmness, – 'I will Robert see,
Know what he wishes, and what I must be;'   340
For James had now discover'd to the maid
His inmost heart, and how he must be paid,
If he his lord would soften, and would hide
The facts that must the culprit's fate decide.
'Go not,' he said, – for she her full intent   345
Proclaim'd – To go she purposed, and she went:
She took a guide, and went with purpose stern
The secret wishes of her friend to learn.
    She saw him fetter'd, full of grief, alone,
Still as the dead, and he suppress'd a groan   350
At her appearance – Now she pray'd for strength;
And the sad couple could converse at length.
It was a scene that shook her to repeat, –
Life fought with love, both powerful, and both sweet.
    'Wilt thou die, Robert, or preserve thy life?   355
Shall I be thine own maid, or James's wife?'
    'His wife! – No! – never will I thee resign –
No, Rachel, no!' – 'Then am I ever thine:
I know thee rash and guilty, – but to thee
I pledged my vow, and thine will ever be: 360

Yet think again, – the life that God has lent
Is thine, but not to cast away. – Consent,
If 't is thy wish; for this I made my way
To thy distress – Command, and I obey.'
    'Perhaps my brother may have gain'd thy heart!' –   365
'Then why this visit, if I wish'd to part?
Was it, ah, man ungrateful! wise to make
Effort like this, to hazard for thy sake
A spotless reputation, and to be
A suppliant to that stern man for thee?   370
But I forgive, – thy spirit has been tried,
And thou art weak, but still thou must decide.
    'I ask'd thy brother, James, would'st thou command,
Without the loving heart, the obedient hand?
I ask thee, Robert, lover, canst thou part   375
With this poor hand, when master of the heart? –
He answer'd, Yes! – I tarry thy reply,
Resign'd with him to live, content with thee to die.'
    Assured of this, with spirits low and tame,
Here life so purchased – there a death of shame;   380
Death once his merriment, but now his dread,
And he with terror thought upon the dead:
'O! sure 't is better to endure the care
And pain of life, than go we know not where.
And is there not the dreaded hell for sin,   385
Or is it only this I feel within?
That, if it lasted, no man would sustain,
But would by any change relieve the pain:
Forgive me, love! it is a loathsome thing
To live not thine; but still this dreaded sting   390
Of death torments me, – I to nature cling. –
Go, and be his – but love him not, be sure –
Go, love him not, – and I will life endure:
He, too, is mortal!' – Rachel deeply sigh'd,
But would no more converse: she had complied,   395
And was no longer free – she was his brother's bride.
    'Farewell!' she said, with kindness, but not fond,
Feeling the pressure of the recent bond,
And put her tenderness apart to give
Advice to one who so desired to live: 400

She then departed, join'd the attending guide,
Reflected – wept – was sad – was satisfied.
  James on her worth and virtue could depend, –
He listen'd gladly to her story's end:
Again he promised Robert's life to save,   405
And claim'd the hand that she in payment gave.
  Robert, when death no longer was in view,
Scorn'd what was done, but could not this undo:
The day appointed for the trial near
He view'd with shame, and not unmix'd with fear, –   410
James might deceive him; and, if not, the schemes
Of men may fail. – Can I depend on James?
  He might; for now the grievous price was paid –
James to the altar led the victim maid,
And gave the trembling girl his faithful word   415
For Robert's safety, and so gave my lord.
  But this, and all the promise hope could give,
Gilded not life, – it was not joy to live;
There was no smile in Rachel, nothing gay,
The hours pass'd off, but never danced away.   420
When drew the gloomy day for trial near
There came a note to Robert, – 'Banish fear!'
  He knew whence safety came, – his terror fled,
But rage and vengeance fill'd his soul instead.
  A stronger fear in his companions rose –   425
The day of trial on their hopes might close:
They had no brothers, none to intercede
For them, their friends suspected, and in need;
Scatter'd, they judged, and could unite no more, –
Not so, – they then were at the prison door.   430
  For some had met who sought the haunts they loved,
And were to pity and to vengeance moved:
Their fellows perish! and they see their fall, –
Why not attempt the steep but guardless wall?
  Attempt was made, his part assign'd each man,   435
And they succeeded in the desperate plan;
In truth, a purposed mercy smoothed their way,
But that they knew not – all triumphant they.
Safe in their well-known haunts, they all prepared
To plan anew, and show how much they dared.   440

With joy the troubled heart of Robert beat,
For life was his, and liberty was sweet;
He look'd around in freedom – in delight?
O! no – his Rachel was another's right!
'Right! – has he then preserved me in the day   445
Of my distress? – He has the lovely pay!
But I no freedom at the slave's request,
The price I paid shall then be repossess'd!
Alas! her virtue and the law prevent,
Force cannot be, and she will not consent;   450
But were that brother gone! – A brother? No!
A circumventor! – and the wretch shall go!
Yet not this hand – How shifts about my mind,
Ungovern'd, guideless, drifting in the wind,
And I am all a tempest, whirl'd around   455
By dreadful thoughts, that fright me and confound; –
I would I saw him on the earth laid low!
I wish the fate, but must not give the blow!'
    So thinks a man when thoughtful; he prefers
A life of peace till man his anger stirs,   460
Then all the efforts of his reason cease,
And he forgets how pleasant was that peace;
Till the wild passions what they seek obtain,
And then he sinks into his calm again.
    Now met the lawless clan, – in secret met,   465
And down at their convivial board were set;
The plans in view to past adventures led,
And the past conflicts present anger bred;
They sigh'd for pleasures gone, they groan'd for heroes dead:
Their ancient stores were rifled, – strong desires   470
Awaked, and wine rekindled latent fires.
    It was a night such bold desires to move,
Strong winds and wintry torrents fill'd the grove;
The crackling boughs that in the forest fell,
The cawing rooks, the cur's affrighten'd yell;   475
The scenes above the wood, the floods below,
Were mix'd, and none the single sound could know;
'Loud blow the blasts,' they cried, 'and call us as they blow.'
    In such a night – and then the heroes told
What had been done in better times of old;   480

How they had conquer'd all opposed to them,
By force in part, in part by stratagem;
And as the tales inflamed the fiery crew,
What had been done they then prepared to do;
"'T is a last night!' they said – the angry blast   485
And roaring floods seem'd answering, ''T is a last!'
　　James knew they met, for he had spies about,
Grave, sober men, whom none presumed to doubt;
For if suspected they had soon been tried
Where fears are evidence, and doubts decide: 490
But these escaped. – Now James companions took,
Sturdy and bold, with terror-stirring look;
He had before, by informations led,
Left the afflicted partner of his bed;
Awaked his men, and through plantations wide,   495
Deep woods, and trackless ling, had been their guide;
And then return'd to wake the pitying wife,
And hear her tender terrors for his life.
　　But in this night a sure informer came,
They were assembled who attack'd his game;   500
Who more than once had through the park made way,
And slain the dappled breed, or vow'd to slay;
The trembling spy had heard the solemn vow,
And need and vengeance both inspired them now.
　　The keeper early had retired to rest   505
For brief repose; – sad thoughts his mind possess'd;
In his short sleep he started from his bed,
And ask'd in fancy's terror, 'Is he dead?'
There was a call below, when James awoke,
Rose from his bed, and arms to aid him took,   510
Not all defensive! – there his helpers stood,
Arm'd like himself, and hastening to the wood.
　　'Why this?' he said, for Rachel pour'd her tears
Profuse, that spoke involuntary fears:
'Sleep, that so early thou for us may'st wake,   515
And we our comforts in return may take;
Sleep, and farewell!' he said, and took his way,
And the sad wife in neither could obey;
She slept not nor well fared, but restless dwelt
On her past life, and past afflictions felt: 520

The man she loved, the brother and the foe
Of him she married! – It had wrought her woe;
Not that she loved, but pitied, and that now
Was, so she fear'd, infringement of her vow:
James too was civil, though she must confess   525
That his was not her kind of happiness;
That he would shoot the man who shot a hare
Was what her timid conscience could not bear;
But still she loved him – wonder'd where he stray'd
In this loud night! and if he were afraid.   530
   More than one hour she thought, and dropping then
In sudden sleep, cried loudly, 'Spare him, men!
And do no murder!' – then awaked she rose,
And thought no more of trying for repose.
   'T was past the dead of night, when every sound   535
That nature mingles might be heard around;
But none from man, – man's feeble voice was hush'd,
Where rivers swelling roar'd, and woods were crush'd;
Hurried by these, the wife could sit no more,
But must the terrors of the night explore.   540
   Softly she left her door, her garden gate,
And seem'd as then committed to her fate;
To every horrid thought and doubt a prey,
She hurried on, already lost her way;
Oft as she glided on in that sad night,   545
She stopp'd to listen, and she look'd for light;
An hour she wander'd, and was still to learn
Aught of her husband's safety or return:
A sudden break of heavy clouds could show
A place she knew not, but she strove to know;   550
Still further on she crept with trembling feet,
With hope a friend, with fear a foe to meet:
And there was something fearful in the sight,
And in the sound of what appear'd to-night;
For now, of night and nervous terror bred,   555
Arose a strong and superstitious dread;
She heard strange noises, and the shapes she saw
Of fancied beings bound her soul in awe.
   The moon was risen, and she sometimes shone
Through thick white clouds, that flew tumultuous on, 560

Passing beneath her with an eagle's speed,
That her soft light imprison'd and then freed;
The fitful glimmering through the hedge-row green
Gave a strange beauty to the changing scene;
And roaring winds and rushing waters lent   565
Their mingled voice that to the spirit went.
    To these she listen'd; but new sounds were heard,
And sight more startling to her soul appear'd;
There were low lengthen'd tones with sobs between,
And near at hand, but nothing yet was seen;   570
She hurried on, and 'Who is there?' she cried,
'A dying wretch!' was from the earth replied.
    It was her lover – was the man she gave,
The price she paid, himself from death to save;
With whom, expiring, she must kneel and pray,   575
While the soul flitted from the shivering clay
That press'd the dewy ground, and bled its life away!
This was the part that duty bad her take,
Instant and ere her feelings were awake;
But now they waked to anguish; there came then,   580
Hurrying with lights, loud-speaking, eager men.
    'And here, my lord, we met – And who is here?
The keeper's wife – Ah! woman, go not near!
There lies the man that was the head of all –
See, in his temples went the fatal ball!   585
And James that instant, who was then our guide,
Felt in his heart the adverse shot and died!
It was a sudden meeting, and the light
Of a dull moon made indistinct our fight;
He foremost fell! – But see, the woman creeps   590
Like a lost thing, that wanders as she sleeps.
See, here her husband's body – but she knows
That other dead! and that her action shows.
Rachel! why look you at your mortal foe? –
She does not hear us – Whither will she go?'   595
    Now, more attentive, on the dead they gazed,
And they were brothers: sorrowing and amazed,
On all a momentary silence came,
A common softness, and a moral shame.
    'Seized you the poachers?' said my lord. – 'They fled, 600

And we pursued not, – one of them was dead,
And one of us: they hurried through the wood,
Two lives were gone, and we no more pursued.
Two lives of men, of valiant brothers lost!
Enough, my lord, do hares and pheasants cost!'   605
    So many thought, and there is found a heart
To dwell upon the deaths on either part;
Since this their morals have been more correct,
The cruel spirit in the place is check'd;
His lordship holds not in such sacred care,   610
Nor takes such dreadful vengeance for a hare;
The smugglers fear, the poacher stands in awe
Of Heaven's own act, and reverence the law;
There was, there is, a terror in the place
That operates on man's offending race;   615
Such acts will stamp their moral on the soul,
And while the bad they threaten and control,
Will to the pious and the humble say,
Yours is the right, the safe, the certain way,
'Tis wisdom to be good, 'tis virtue to obey.   620
    So Rachel thinks, the pure, the good, the meek,
Whose outward acts the inward purpose speak;
As men will children at their sports behold,
And smile to see them, though unmoved and cold,
Smile at the recollected games, and then   625
Depart and mix in the affairs of men:
So Rachel looks upon the world, and sees
It cannot longer pain her, longer please,
But just detain the passing thought, or cause
A gentle smile of pity or applause;   630
And then the recollected soul repairs
Her slumbering hope, and heeds her own affairs.

Silford Hall; or The Happy Day

Within a village, many a mile from town,
A place of small resort and no renown; –
Save that it form'd a way, and gave a name
To Silford Hall, it made no claim to fame; –
It was the gain of some, the pride of all,   5
That travellers stopt to ask for Silford Hall.
 Small as it was, the place could boast a School,
In which Nathaniel Perkin bore the rule.
Not mark'd for learning deep, or talents rare,
But for his varying tasks and ceaseless care;   10
Some forty boys, the sons of thrifty men,
He taught to read, and part to use the pen;
While, by more studious care, a favourite few
Increased his pride – for if the Scholar knew
Enough for praise, say what the Teacher's due? –   15
These to his presence, slates in hand, moved on,
And a grim smile their feats in figures won.
This Man of Letters woo'd in early life
The Vicar's maiden, whom he made his wife.
She too can read, as by her song she proves –   20
The song Nathaniel made about their loves:
Five rosy girls, and one fair boy, increased
The Father's care, whose labours seldom ceased.
No day of rest was his. If, now and then,
His boys for play laid by the book and pen,   25
For Lawyer Slow there was some deed to write,
Or some young farmer's letter to indite,
Or land to measure, or, with legal skill,
To frame some yeoman's widow's peevish will;
And on the Sabbath, – when his neighbours drest,   30
To hear their duties, and to take their rest –
Then, when the Vicar's periods ceased to flow,
Was heard Nathaniel, in his seat below.
 Such were his labours; but the time is come
When his son Peter clears the hours of gloom,   35
And brings him aid: though yet a boy, he shares

In staid Nathaniel's multifarious cares.
A king his father, he, a prince, has rule –
The first of subjects, viceroy of the school:
But though a prince within that realm he reigns,   40
Hard is the part his duteous soul sustains.
He with his Father, o'er the furrow'd land,
Draws the long chain in his uneasy hand,
And neatly forms at home, what there they rudely plann'd.
Content, for all his labour, if he gains   45
Some words of praise, and sixpence for his pains.
Thus many a hungry day the Boy has fared,
And would have ask'd a dinner, had he dared.
When boys are playing, he, for hours of school
Has sums to set, and copy-books to rule;   50
When all are met, for some sad dunce afraid,
He, by allowance, lends his timely aid –
Taught at the student's failings to connive,
Yet keep his Father's dignity alive:
For ev'n Nathaniel fears, and might offend,   55
If too severe, the farmer, now his friend;
Or her, that farmer's lady, who well knows
Her boy is bright, and needs nor threats nor blows.
This seem'd to Peter hard; and he was loth,
T' obey and rule, and have the cares of both –   60
To miss the master's dignity, and yet,
No portion of the school-boy's play to get.
To him the Fiend, as once to Launcelot, cried,
'Run from thy wrongs!' – 'Run where?' his fear replied:
  'Run!' – said the Tempter, 'if but hard thy fare,   65
Hard is it now – it *may* be mended there.'
  But still, though tempted, he refused to part,
And felt the Mother clinging at his heart.
Nor this alone – he, in that weight of care,
Had help, and bore it as a man should bear.   70
A drop of comfort in his cup was thrown;
It was his treasure, and it was his own.
His Father's shelves contained a motley store
Of letter'd wealth; and this he might explore.
A part his mother in her youth had gain'd,   75
A part Nathaniel from his club obtain'd,

And part – a well-worn kind – from sire to son remain'd.
  He sought his Mother's hoard, and there he found
Romance in sheets, and poetry unbound;
Soft Tales of Love, which never damsel read,   80
But tears of pity stain'd her virgin bed.
There were Jane Shore and Rosamond the Fair,
And humbler heroines frail as these were there;
There was a tale of one forsaken Maid,
Who till her death the work of vengeance stay'd;   85
Her Lover, then at sea, while round him stood
A dauntless crew, the angry ghost pursued;
In a small boat, without an oar or sail,
She came to call him, nor would force avail,
Nor prayer; but, conscience-stricken, down he leapt,   90
And o'er his corse the closing billows slept;
All vanish'd then! but of the crew were some,
Wondering whose ghost would on the morrow come.
  A learned Book was there, and in it schemes
How to cast Fortunes and interpret Dreams;   95
Ballads were there of Lover's bliss or bale,
The Kitchen Story, and the Nursery Tale.
His hungry mind disdain'd not humble food,
And read with relish keen of Robin Hood;
Of him, all-powerful made by magic gift,   100
And Giants slain – of mighty Hickerthrift;
Through Crusoe's Isle delighted had he stray'd,
Nocturnal visits had to witches paid,
Gliding through haunted scenes, enraptured and afraid.
  A loftier shelf with real books was graced,   105
Bound, or part bound, and ranged in comely taste;
Books of high mark, the mind's more solid food,
Which some might think the owner understood;
But Fluxions, Sections, Algebraic lore,
Our Peter left for others to explore,   110
And quickly turning to a favourite kind,
Found, what rejoiced him at his heart to find.
  Sir Walter wrote not then, or He by whom
Such gain and glory to Sir Walter come –
That Fairy-Helper, by whose secret aid,   115
Such views of life are to the world convey'd –

As inspiration known in after-times,
The sole assistant in his prose or rhymes.
But there were fictions wild that please the boy,
Which men, too, read, condemn, reject, enjoy –   120
Arabian Nights, and Persian Tales were there,
One volume each, and both the worse for wear;
There by Quarles' Emblems, Esop's Fables stood,
The coats in tatters, and the cuts in wood.
There, too, 'The English History,' by the pen   125
Of Doctor Coote, and other learned men,
In numbers, sixpence each; by these was seen,
And highly prized, the Monthly Magazine; –
Not such as now will men of taste engage,
But the cold gleanings of a former age,   130
Scraps cut from sermons, scenes removed from plays,
With heads of heroes famed in Tyburn's palmy days.
    The rest we pass – though Peter pass'd them not,
But here his cares and labours all forgot:
Stain'd, torn, and blotted every noble page,   135
Stood the chief poets of a former age –
And of the present; not their works complete,
But in such portions as on bulks we meet,
The refuse of the shops, thrown down upon the street.
There Shakspeare, Spenser, Milton found a place,   140
With some a nameless, some a shameless race,
Which many a weary walker resting reads,
And, pondering o'er the short relief, proceeds,
While others lingering pay the written sum,
Half loth, but longing for delight to come.   145
    Of the Youth's morals we would something speak;
Taught by his Mother what to shun or seek:
She show'd the heavenly way, and in his youth,
Press'd on his yielding mind the Gospel truth,
How weak is man, how much to ill inclined,   150
And where his help is placed, and how to find.
These words of weight sank deeply in his breast,
And awful Fear and holy Hope imprest.
He shrank from vice, and at the startling view,
As from an adder in his path, withdrew.   155
All else was cheerful. Peter's easy mind

To the gay scenes of village-life inclined.
The lark that soaring sings his notes of joy,
Was not more lively than th' awaken'd boy.
Yet oft with this a softening sadness dwelt,   160
While, feeling thus, he marvell'd why he felt.
'I am not sorry,' said the Boy, 'but still,
The tear will drop – I wonder why it will!'
   His books, his walks, his musing, morn and eve,
Gave such impressions as such minds receive;   165
And with his moral and religious views
Wove the wild fancies of an Infant-Muse,
Inspiring thoughts that he could not express,
Obscure sublime! his secret happiness.
Oft would he strive for words, and oft begin   170
To frame in verse the views he had within;
But ever fail'd: for how can words explain
The unform'd ideas of a teeming brain?
   Such was my Hero, whom I would portray
In one exploit – the Hero of a Day.   175
   At six miles' distance from his native town
Stood Silford Hall, a seat of much renown –
Computed miles, such weary travellers ride,
When they in chance wayfaring men confide.
Beauty and grandeur were within; around,   180
Lawn, wood, and water; the delicious ground
Had parks where deer disport, had fields where game abound.
Fruits of all tastes in spacious gardens grew;
And flowers of every scent and every hue,
That native in more favour'd climes arise,   185
Are here protected from th' inclement skies.
   To this fair place, with mingled pride and shame
This lad of learning without knowledge came –
Shame for his conscious ignorance – and pride
To this fair seat in this gay style to ride.   190
   The cause that brought him was a small account,
His father's due, and he must take the amount,
And sign a stamp'd receipt! this done, he might
Look all around him, and enjoy the sight.
   So far to walk was, in his mother's view,   195
More than her darling Peter ought to do;

Peter indeed knew more, but he would hide
His better knowledge, for he wish'd to ride;
So had his father's nag, a beast so small,
That if he fell, he had not far to fall.   200
    His fond and anxious mother in his best,
Her darling child for the occasion drest:
All in his coat of green she clothed her boy,
And stood admiring with a mother's joy:
Large was it made and long, as meant to do   205
For Sunday-service, when he older grew –
Not brought in daily use in one year's wear or two.
White was his waistcoat, and what else he wore
Had clothed the lamb or parent ewe before.
In all the mother show'd her care or skill;   210
A riband black she tied beneath his frill;
Gave him his stockings, white as driven snow,
And bad him heed the miry way below;
On the black varnish of the comely shoe,
Shone the large buckle of a silvery hue.   215
Boots he had worn, had he such things possest –
But bootless grief! – he was full proudly drest;
Full proudly look'd, and light he was of heart,
When thus for Silford Hall prepared to start.
    Nathaniel's self with joy the stripling eyed,   220
And gave a shilling with a father's pride;
Rules of politeness too with pomp he gave,
And show'd the lad how scholars should behave.
    Ere yet he left her home, the Mother told –
For she had seen – what things he should behold.   225
There, she related, her young eyes had view'd
Stone figures shaped like naked flesh and blood,
Which, in the hall and up the gallery placed,
Were proofs, they told her, of a noble taste;
Nor she denied – but, in a public hall,   230
Her judgment taken, she had clothed them all.
There, too, were station'd, each upon its seat,
Half forms of men, without their hands and feet;
These and what more within that hall might be
She saw, and oh! how long'd her son to see!   235
Yet could he hope to view that noble place,

Who dared not look the porter in the face?
   Forth went the pony, and the rider's knees
Cleaved to her sides – he did not ride with ease;
One hand a whip, and one a bridle held,   240
In case the pony falter'd or rebell'd.
   The village boys beheld him as he pass'd,
And looks of envy on the hero cast;
But he was meek, nor let his pride appear,
Nay, truth to speak, he felt a sense of fear,   245
Lest the rude beast, unmindful of the rein,
Should take a fancy to turn back again.
   He found, and wonder 't is he found, his way,
The orders many that he must obey:
'Now to the right, then left, and now again   250
Directly onward, through the winding lane;
Then, half way o'er the common, by the mill,
Turn from the cottage and ascend the hill,
Then – spare the pony, boy! – as you ascend –
You see the Hall, and that's your journey's end.'   255
   Yes, he succeeded, not remembering aught
Of this advice, but by his pony taught.
Soon as he doubted he the bridle threw
On the steed's neck, and said – 'Remember you!'
For oft the creature had his father borne,   260
Sound on his way, and safe on his return.
So he succeeded, and the modest youth
Gave praise, where praise had been assign'd by truth.
   His business done, – for fortune led his way
To him whose office was such debts to pay,   265
The farmer-bailiff, but he saw no more
Than a small room, with bare and oaken floor,
A desk with books thereon – he'd seen such things before;
'Good day!' he said, but linger'd as he spoke
'Good day,' and gazed about with serious look;   270
Then slowly moved, and then delay'd awhile,
In dumb dismay which raised a lordly smile
In those who eyed him – then again moved on,
As all might see, unwilling to be gone.
   While puzzled thus, and puzzling all about,   275
Involved, absorb'd, in some bewildering doubt,

A lady enter'd, Madam Johnson call'd,
Within whose presence stood the lad appall'd.
A learned Lady this, who knew the names
Of all the pictures in the golden frames;   280
Could every subject, every painter, tell,
And on their merits and their failures dwell;
And if perchance there was a slight mistake –
These the most knowing on such matters make.
     'And what dost mean, my pretty lad?' she cried,   285
'Dost stay or go?' – He first for courage tried,
Then for fit words, – then boldly he replied,
That he 'would give a hundred pounds, if so
He had them, all about that house to go;
For he had heard that it contain'd such things   290
As never house could boast, except the king's.'
     The ruling Lady, smiling, said, 'In truth
Thou shalt behold them all, my pretty youth.
Tom! first the creature to the stable lead,
Let it be fed; and you, my child, must feed;   295
For three good hours must pass e'er dinner come,' –
'Supper,' thought he, 'she means, our time at home.'
     First was he feasted to his heart's content,
Then, all in rapture, with the Lady went;
Through rooms immense, and galleries wide and tall,   300
He walk'd entranced – he breathed in Silford Hall.
     Now could he look on that delightful place,
The glorious dwelling of a princely race;
His vast delight was mixed with equal awe,
There was such magic in the things he saw.   305
Oft standing still, with open mouth and eyes,
Turn'd here and there, alarm'd as one who tries
T'escape from something strange, that would before him rise.
The wall would part, and beings without name
Would come – for such to his adventures came.   310
Hence undefined and solemn terror press'd
Upon his mind, and all his powers possess'd.
All he had read of magic, every charm,
Were he alone, might come and do him harm:
But his gaze rested on his friendly guide –   315
'I'm safe,' he thought, 'so long as you abide.'

In one large room was found a bed of state –
'And can they soundly sleep beneath such weight,
Where they may figures in the night explore,
Form'd by the dim light dancing on the floor   320
From the far window; mirrors broad and high
Doubling each terror to the anxious eye? –
'T is strange,' thought Peter, 'that such things produce
No fear in *her*; but there is much in use.'
   On that reflecting brightness, passing by,   325
The Boy one instant fix'd his restless eye –
And saw himself: he had before descried
His face in one his mother's store supplied;
But here he could his whole dimensions view,
From the pale forehead to the jet-black shoe.   330
Passing he look'd, and looking, grieved to pass
From the fair figure smiling in the glass.
'T was so Narcissus saw the boy advance
In the dear fount, and met th' admiring glance
So loved – But no! our happier boy admired,   335
Not the slim form, but what the form attired, –
The riband, shirt, and frill, all pure and clean,
The white ribb'd stockings, and the coat of green.
   The Lady now appear'd to move away –
And this was threat'ning; for he dared not stay,   340
Lost and alone; but earnestly he pray'd –
'Oh! do not leave me – I am not afraid,
But 't is so lonesome; I shall never find
My way alone, no better than the blind.'
   The Matron kindly to the Boy replied,   345
'Trust in my promise, I will be thy guide.'
Then to the Chapel moved the friendly pair,
And well for Peter that his guide was there!
Dim, silent, solemn was the scene – he felt
The cedar's power, that so unearthly smelt;   350
And then the stain'd, dark, narrow windows threw
Strange, partial beams on pulpit, desk, and pew:
Upon the altar, glorious to behold,
Stood a vast pair of candlesticks in gold!
With candles tall, and large, and firm, and white,   355
Such as the halls of giant-kings would light.

There was an organ, too, but now unseen;
A long black curtain served it for a skreen;
Not so the clock, that both by night and day,
Click'd the short moments as they pass'd away.   360
  'Is this a church? and does the parson read' –
Said Peter – 'here? – I mean a church indeed.' –
'Indeed it is, or as a church is used,'
Was the reply, – and Peter deeply mused,
Not without awe. His sadness to dispel,   365
They sought the gallery, and then all was well.
  Yet enter'd there, although so clear his mind
From every fear substantial and defined,
Yet there remain'd some touch of native fear –
Of something awful to the eye and ear –   370
A ghostly voice might sound – a ghost itself appear.
  There noble Pictures fill'd his mind with joy –
He gazed and thought, and was no more the boy;
And Madam heard him speak, with some surprise,
Of heroes known to him from histories.   375
He knew the actors in the deeds of old, –
He could the Roman marvels all unfold.
He to his guide a theme for wonder grew,
At once so little and so much he knew –
Little of what was passing every day,   380
And much of that which long had pass'd away; –
So like a man, and yet so like a child,
That his good friend stood wond'ring as she smiled.
  The Scripture Pieces caused a serious awe,
And he with reverence look'd on all he saw;   385
His pious wonder he express'd aloud,
And at the Saviour Form devoutly bow'd.
  Portraits he pass'd, admiring; but with pain
Turn'd from some objects, nor would look again.
He seem'd to think that something wrong was done,   390
When crimes were shown he blush'd to look upon.
Not so his guide – 'What youth is that?' she cried,
'That handsome stripling at the lady's side;
Can you inform me how the youth is named?'
He answer'd, 'Joseph;' but he look'd ashamed.   395
'Well, and what then? Had you been Joseph, boy!

Would you have been so peevish and so coy?'
Our hero answer'd, with a glowing face,
'His mother told him he should pray for grace.'
A transient cloud o'ercast the matron's brow;   400
She seem'd disposed to laugh – but knew not how;
Silent awhile, then placid she appear'd –
''T is but a child,' she thought, and all was clear'd.
    No – laugh she could not; still, the more she sought
To hide her thoughts, the more of his she caught.   405
A hundred times she had these pictures named,
And never felt perplex'd, disturb'd, ashamed;
Yet now the feelings of a lad so young
Call'd home her thoughts and paralysed her tongue.
She pass'd the offensive pictures silent by,   410
With one reflecting, self-reproving sigh;
Reasoning how habit will the mind entice
To approach and gaze upon the bounds of vice,
As men, by custom, from some cliff's vast height,
Look pleased, and make their danger their delight.   415
'Come, let us on! – see there a Flemish view,
A Country Fair, and all as Nature true.
See there the merry creatures, great and small,
Engaged in drinking, gaming, dancing all,
Fiddling or fighting – all in drunken joy!' –   420
'But is this Nature?' said the wondering Boy.
    'Be sure it is! and those Banditti there –
Observe the faces, forms, the eyes, the air:
See rage, revenge, remorse, disdain, despair!'
    'And is that Nature, too?' the stripling cried. –   425
'Corrupted Nature,' said the serious guide.
    She then display'd her knowledge. – 'That, my dear,
Is call'd a Titian, this a Guido here,
And yon a Claude – you see that lovely light,
So soft and solemn, neither day nor night.'   430
    'Yes!' quoth the Boy, 'and there is just the breeze,
That curls the water, and that fans the trees;
The ships that anchor in that pleasant bay
All look so safe and quiet – Claude, you say?'
    On a small picture Peter gazed and stood   435
In admiration – ''t was so dearly good.'

'For how much money think you, then, my Lad,
Is such a "dear good picture" to be had?
'T is a famed master's work – a Gerard Dow,
At least the seller told the buyer so.'   440
   'I tell the price!' quoth Peter – 'I as soon
Could tell the price of pictures in the moon;
But I have heard, when the great race was done,
How much was offer'd for the horse that won.' –
   'A thousand pounds: but, look the country round,   445
And, may be, ten such horses might be found;
While, ride or run where'ver you choose to go,
You'll nowhere find so fine a Gerard Dow.'
   'If this be true,' says Peter, 'then, of course,
You'd rate the picture higher than the horse.'   450
   'Why, thou'rt a reasoner, Boy!' the lady cried;
'But see that Infant on the other side;
'T is by Sir Joshua. Did you ever see
A Babe so charming?' – 'No, indeed,' said he;
'I wonder how he could that look invent,   455
That seems so sly, and yet so innocent.'
   In this long room were various Statues seen,
And Peter gazed thereon with awe-struck mien.
   'Why look so earnest, Boy?' – 'Because they bring
To me a story of an awful thing.' –   460
   'Tell then thy story.' – He who never stay'd
For words or matter, instantly obey'd. –
   'A holy pilgrim to a city sail'd,
Where every sin o'er sinful men prevail'd;
Who, when he landed, look'd in every street,   465
As he was wont, a busy crowd to meet;
But now of living beings found he none,
Death had been there, and turn'd them all to stone;
All in an instant, as they were employ'd,
Was life in every living man destroy'd –   470
The rich, the poor, the timid, and the bold,
Made in a moment such as we behold.'
   'Come, my good lad, you've yet a room to see.
Are you awake?' – 'I am amazed,' said he;
'I know they're figures form'd by human skill,   475
But 't is so awful, and this place so still!

'And what is this?' said Peter, who had seen
A long wide table, with its cloth of green,
Its net-work pockets, and its studs of gold –
For such they seem'd, and precious to behold.   480
There too were ivory balls, and one was red,
Laid with long sticks upon the soft green bed,
And printed tables, on the wall beside –
'Oh! what are these?' the wondering Peter cried.
     'This, my good lad, is call'd the Billiard-room,'   485
Answer'd his guide, 'and here the gentry come,
And with these maces and these cues they play,
At their spare time, or in a rainy day.'
     'And what this chequer'd box? – for play, I guess?' –
'You judge it right; 't is for the game of Chess.   490
There! take your time, examine what you will,
There's King, Queen, Knight, – it is a game of skill:
And these are Bishops; you the difference see.' –
'What! do they make a game of *them*?' quoth he. –
'Bishops, like Kings,' she said, 'are here but names;   495
Not that I answer for their Honours' games.'
     All round the house did Peter go, and found
Food for his wonder all the house around.
There guns of various bore, and rods, and lines,
And all that man for deed of death designs,   500
In beast, or bird, or fish, or worm, or fly –
Life in these last must means of death supply;
The living bait is gorged, and both the victims die.
'God gives man leave his creatures to destroy.' –
'What! for his sport?' replied the pitying Boy. –   505
'Nay,' said the Lady, 'why the sport condemn?
As die they must, 't is much the same to them.'
Peter had doubts; but with so kind a friend,
He would not on a dubious point contend.
     Much had he seen, and every thing he saw   510
Excited pleasure not unmix'd with awe.
Leaving each room, he turn'd as if once more
To enjoy the pleasure that he felt before –
'What then must their possessors feel? how grand
And happy they who can such joys command!   515
For they may pleasures all their lives pursue,

The winter pleasures, and the summer's too –
Pleasures for every hour in every day –
Oh! how their time must pass in joy away!'
So Peter said. – Replied the courteous Dame: 520
'What you call pleasure scarcely owns the name.
The very changes of amusement prove
There's nothing that deserves a lasting love.
They hunt, they course, they shoot, they fish, they game;
The objects vary, though the end the same –   525
A search for that which flies them; no, my Boy!
'T is not enjoyment, 't is pursuit of joy.'
    Peter was thoughtful – thinking, What! not these,
Who can command, or purchase, what they please –
Whom many serve, who only speak the word,   530
And they have all that earth or seas afford –
All that can charm the mind and please the eye –
And *they* not happy! – but I'll ask her why.
    So Peter ask'd. – ''T is not,' she said, 'for us,
Their Honours' inward feelings to discuss;   535
But if they're happy, they would still confess
'T is not these things that make their happiness.
    'Look from this window! at his work behold
Yon gardener's helper – he is poor and old,
He not one thing of all you see can call   540
His own; but, haply, he o'erlooks them all.
Hear him! he whistles through his work, or stops
But to admire his labours and his crops:
To-day as every former day he fares,
And for the morrow has nor doubts nor cares;   545
Pious and cheerful, proud when he can please,
Judge if Joe Tompkin wants such things as these.
    'Come, let us forward!' and she walk'd in haste
To a large room, itself a work of taste,
But chiefly valued for the works that drew   550
The eyes of Peter – this indeed was new,
Was most imposing – Books of every kind
Were there disposed, the food for every mind.
With joy perplex'd, round cast he wondering eyes,
Still in his joy, and dumb in his surprise.   555
    Above, beneath, around, on every side,

Of every form and size were Books descried;
Like Bishop Hatto, when the rats drew near,
And war's new dangers waked his guilty fear,
When thousands came beside, behind, before,   560
And up and down came on ten thousand more;
A tail'd and whisker'd army, each with claws
As sharp as needles, and with teeth like saws, –
So fill'd with awe, and wonder in his looks,
Stood Peter, 'midst this multitude of Books;   565
But guiltless he and fearless; yet he sigh'd
To think what treasures were to him denied.
     But wonder ceases on continued view;
And the Boy sharp for close inspection grew.
Prints on the table he at first survey'd,   570
Then to the Books his full attention paid.
At first, from tome to tome, as fancy led,
He view'd the binding, and the titles read;
Lost in delight, and with his freedom pleased,
Then three huge folios from their shelf he seized;   575
Fixing on one, with prints of every race,
Of beast and bird most rare in every place, –
Serpents, the giants of their tribe, whose prey
Are giants too – a wild ox once a day;
Here the fierce tiger, and the desert's kings,   580
And all that move on feet, or fins, or wings –
Most rare and strange; a second volume told
Of battles dire, and dreadful to behold,
On sea or land, and fleets dispersed in storms;
A third has all creative fancy forms, –   585
Hydra and dire chimera, deserts rude,
And ruins grand, enriching solitude:
Whatever was, or was supposed to be,
Saw Peter here, and still desired to see.
     Again he look'd, but happier had he been,   590
That Book of Wonders he had never seen;
For there were tales of men of wicked mind,
And how the Foe of Man deludes mankind.
Magic and murder every leaf bespread –
Enchanted halls, and chambers of the dead,   595
And ghosts that haunt the scenes where once the victims bled.

Just at this time, when Peter's heart began
To admit the fear that shames the valiant man,
He paused – but why? 'Here's one my guard to be;
When thus protected, none can trouble me:' –   600
Then rising look'd he round, and lo! alone was he.
    Three ponderous doors, with locks of shining brass,
Seem'd to invite the trembling Boy to pass;
But fear forbad, till fear itself supplied
The place of courage, and at length he tried.   605
He grasp'd the key – Alas! though great his need,
The key turn'd not, the bolt would not recede.
Try then again; for what will not distress?
Again he tried, and with the same success.
Yet one remains, remains untried one door –   610
A failing hope, for two had fail'd before;
But a bold prince, with fifty doors in sight,
Tried forty-nine before he found the right;
Before he mounted on the brazen horse,
And o'er the walls pursued his airy course.   615
So his cold hand on this last key he laid:
'Now turn,' said he; the treacherous bolt obey'd –
The door receded – bringing full in view
The dim, dull chapel, pulpit, desk, and pew.
    It was not right – it would have vex'd a saint;   620
And Peter's anger rose above restraint.
'Was this her love,' he cried, 'to bring me here,
Among the dead, to die myself with fear!' –
For Peter judged, with monuments around,
The dead must surely in the place be found: –   625
'With cold to shiver, and with hunger pine –
"We'll see the rooms," she said, "before we dine;"
And spake so kind! That window gives no light:
Here is enough the boldest man to fright;
It hardly now is day, and soon it will be night.'   630
    Deeply he sigh'd, nor from his heart could chase
The dread of dying in that dismal place;
Anger and sorrow in his bosom strove,
And banish'd all that yet remain'd of love;
When soon despair had seized the trembling Boy,   635
But hark, a voice! the sound of peace and joy.

'Where art thou, lad?' – 'Oh! here am I, in doubt,
And sorely frighten'd – can you let me out?'
'Oh! yes, my child; it was indeed a sin,
Forgetful as I was, to bolt you in.   640
I left you reading, and from habit lock'd
The door behind me, but in truth am shock'd
To serve you thus; but we will make amends
For such mistake. Come, cheerly, we are friends.'
'Oh! yes,' said Peter, quite alive to be   645
So kindly used, and have so much to see,
And having so much seen; his way he spied,
Forgot his peril, and rejoin'd his guide.
Now all beheld, his admiration raised,
The lady thank'd, her condescension praised,   650
And fix'd the hour for dinner, forth the Boy
Went in a tumult of o'erpowering joy,
To view the gardens, and what more was found
In the wide circuit of that spacious ground,
Till, with his thoughts bewilder'd, and oppress'd   655
With too much feeling, he inclined to rest.
Then in the park he sought its deepest shade,
By trees more aged than the mansion made,
That ages stood; and there unseen a brook
Ran not unheard, and thus our traveller spoke, –   660
'I am so happy, and have such delight,
I cannot bear to see another sight;
It wearies one like work;' and so, with deep
Unconscious sigh – he laid him down to sleep.
Thus he reclining slept, and, oh! the joy   665
That in his dreams possess'd the happy boy, –
Composed of all he knew, and all he read,
Heard, or conceived, the living and the dead.
The Caliph Haroun, walking forth by night
To see young David and Goliath fight,   670
Rose on his passive fancy – then appear'd
The fleshless forms of beings scorn'd or fear'd
By just or evil men – the baneful race
Of spirits restless, borne from place to place:
Rivers of blood from conquer'd armies ran,   675
The flying steed was by, the marble man;

Then danced the fairies round their pygmy queen,
And their feet twinkled on the dewy green,
All in the moon-beams' glory. As they fled,
The mountain loadstone rear'd its fatal head,   680
And drew the iron-bolted ships on shore,
Where he distinctly heard the billows roar, –
Mix'd with a living voice of – 'Youngster, sleep no more,
But haste to dinner.' Starting from the ground,
The waking boy obey'd that welcome sound.   685
　　He went and sat, with equal shame and pride,
A welcome guest at Madam Johnson's side.
At his right hand was Mistress Kitty placed,
And Lucy, maiden sly, the stripling faced.
Then each the proper seat at table took –   690
Groom, butler, footman, laundress, coachman, cook;
For all their station and their office knew,
Nor sat as rustics or the rabble do.
　　The Youth to each the due attention paid,
And hob-or-nob'd with Lady Charlotte's maid;   695
With much respect each other they address'd,
And all encouraged their enchanted guest.
Wine, fruit, and sweetmeats closed repast so long,
And Mistress Flora sang an opera song.
　　Such was the Day the happy Boy had spent,   700
And forth delighted from the Hall he went:
Bowing his thanks, he mounted on his steed,
More largely fed than he was wont to feed;
And well for Peter that his pony knew
From whence he came, the road he should pursue;   705
For the young rider had his mind estranged
From all around, disturb'd and disarranged,
In pleasing tumult, in a dream of bliss.
Enjoy'd but seldom in a world like this.
　　But though the pleasures of the Day were past, –   710
For lively pleasures are not form'd to last, –
And though less vivid they became, less strong,
Through life they lived, and were enjoy'd as long
So deep the impression of that happy Day,
Not time nor cares could wear it all away;   715
Ev'n to the last, in his declining years,

He told of all his glories, all his fears.
   How blithely forward in that morn he went,
How blest the hours in that fair palace spent,
How vast that Mansion, sure for monarch plann'd,   720
The rooms so many, and yet each so grand, –
Millions of books in one large hall were found,
And glorious pictures every room around;
Beside that strangest of the wonders there,
That house itself contain'd a house of prayer.   725
   He told of park and wood, of sun and shade,
And how the lake below the lawn was made:
He spake of feasting such as never boy,
Taught in his school, was fated to enjoy –
Of ladies' maids as ladies' selves who dress'd,   730
And her, his friend, distinguish'd from the rest,
By grandeur in her look, and state that she possess'd.
He pass'd not one; his grateful mind o'erflow'd
With sense of all he felt, and they bestow'd.
   He spake of every office, great or small,   735
Within, without, and spake with praise of all –
So pass'd the happy Boy, that Day at Silford Hall.

Notes

Unless stated otherwise, texts of all poems and extracts are taken from: *The Poetical Works of the Rev. George Crabbe: with his Letters and Journals, and his Life, by his Son* [George Crabbe jun.], 8 vols (London: John Murray, 1834].

Crabbe's epigraphs, synopses and footnotes have been omitted; proper names printed in capitals or italics have been regularized; inverted commas are found only at the beginning and end of speeches, rather than at the start of every line of speech; and to save space, paragraphs have been closed up. Obvious misprints have been silently corrected.

p. 3 *Inebriety*: First published anonymously in 1775, in Ipswich. The poem is in three parts. The 1834 text is unsatisfactory: the text printed here is taken from *George Crabbe: Poems*, ed. A. W. Ward, 3 vols (Cambridge: CUP, 1905–07). **Part the First:** Crabbe imitates Pope, especially the 'Dunciad' and the 'Essay on Man'. **l.39 'rrack:** arrack, an alcoholic drink. **l.41 Colin:** traditional name for a rustic. **l.54 Hel'con:** Helicon, mountain in Greece, home of the Muses. **l.59 Lucina:** the moon. **l.110 sots in crape:** drunken clergymen. **l.118 Flaminius:** a priest. **l.128 God like Egypt's:** Osiris.

p.7 *Ye Gentle Gales*: Written *c.* 1776; first published in 1834.

p.7 *The Comparison*: Written 1778; first published in 1834.

p.8 *The Village*: First published in 1783; reprinted with alterations and additions in 1807, which is the basis for the 1834 text. The poem is in two Books. *from* **Book One:** Lines **1–92** correspond to **ll.39–130** in 1834; **ll.93–211** to **ll.228–346** in 1834. **l.59 Ajax:** mythical Greek hero of the Trojan War. **l.76 yearly dinner:** this would follow the annual election of parish officers; **septennial bribe:** general elections had to take place every seven years. **l.168 'passing rich with forty pounds a year':** Oliver Goldsmith, 'The Deserted Village', 142. **l.205 mingled relics:** remains of paupers buried in a common grave. *from* **Book Two:** These are **ll.1–106** in 1834. **l.50 Cynthia:** the Greek goddess Artemis (Roman Diana), usually personified as a virgin huntress. **l.84 doubts 'twixt war and wife:** the father must either marry the pregnant girl, or enlist in the army or militia.

p.16 From *The Newspaper*: First published in 1785. This extract reprints lines **1—106** of the poem. **l.20 Cibber:** Colley Cibber (1671–1757), actor, playwright and poet, the hero of Pope's revised 'Dunciad', Poet Laureate from 1730; **Settle:** Elkanah Settle (1684–1724), dramatist and poet. **l.22 once-triumphant Nine:** the nine Muses. **ll.54–58 The Herald . . . Posts again:** London newspapers. **l.63 Lloyd's:** a coffee-house. **l.64 Alley:** Head Alley. **l.69 ephemeras:** mayflies. **l.77 sainted Monitor:** *British Gazette and Sunday Monitor,* the first Sunday newspaper. **l.92 Woodfall:** Henry Sampson Woodfall (1739–1805), editor of the *Public Advertiser.*

p.20 *The Parish Register*: First published in 1807, the poem is divided into three parts: 'Baptisms', 'Marriages', 'Burials'. ***from* Part Two: Marriages:** These lines correspond to **ll.502–73** in 1834. ***from* Part Three: Burials:** These lines correspond to **ll.312–412** in 1834. **l.12 a pea-green Joseph:** a lady's greatcoat.

p.25 *The Borough*: First published in 1810, it is divided into twenty-four Letters. The unnamed Borough is not Aldeburgh, but a montage of the real and the imaginary to which Aldeburgh contributed. ***General Description*.** Letter One. **l.9 he, who sang so well the Grecian fleet:** Homer. **l.52 Hoys:** small coasting vessels, rigged as sloops; **pinks:** ships with a very narrow stern; **brigantines:** small, two-masted merchant ships; **snows:** vessels with two masts and a third, smaller mast. **l.134 'Like a tall bully, lifts its head and lies':** adapted from Alexander Pope, 'To Allen Lord Bathurst. Of the Use of Riches', *Moral Essays*, Epistle 3, 340. **l.150 gale:** bog-myrtle, or candleberry.

p.33 *Peter Grimes*: Letter Twenty-Two. The original of Grimes was an old fisherman of Aldeburgh, who employed a succession of London apprentices, all of whom disappeared in suspicious circumstances. Crabbe's Grimes differs greatly from Britten's conception of the character. **l.195 golden-eye:** a sea-duck.

p.42 *Prisons*: Letter Twenty-Three. **l.155 Homer! nay Pope!:** a reference to Pope's translations of Homer's *Iliad* (1715–20) and *Odyssey* (1725–26). **ll.167–8 Now as we . . . meads of asphodel:** adapted from Pope's 'Ode for Music on St Cecilia's Day', 74–5. **l.169 the poet:** Homer, describing Odysseus' descent into Hades.

p.51 *The Frank Courtship*: First published in 1812, as Tale Six of *Tales*. **l.11 Sarah call'd Abraham Lord!:** see 1 Peter 3:6. **l.34 their Sovereign:** Charles I (1600–49). **l.39 Cromwell:** Oliver Cromwell (1599–1658), Lord Protector 1653–58. **l.58 bold Protector:** Cromwell. **l.61 the House:** parliament. **l.74 Gretna-Green:** village on Scottish border where eloping couples could marry.

p.64 *The Magnet*: Written *c.* 1814; first published in 1834.

p.64 *Satire*: Written 1818; first published in 1834.

p.65 *Smugglers and Poachers*: First published in 1819, as Book Twenty-One of *Tales of the Hall*.

p.82 *Silford Hall, or The Happy Day*: First published in 1834, as Tale One of *Posthumous Tales*. Silford Hall appears to draw on Crabbe's memories of Cheveley and of Belvoir Castle. **ll.63–4: To him the Fiend . . . from thy wrongs!:** see Launcelot Gobbo's opening speech in *The Merchant of Venice*, II ii. **l.82 Jane Shore:** (died *c.*1527) mistress of Edward IV; **Rosamond the Fair:** Rosamond Clifford (died *c.*1176), mistress of Henry II. **l.99 Robin Hood:** legendary medieval outlaw. **l.101 Hickerthrift:** Tom Hickathrift, legendary Saxon giant-killer from the Isle of Ely. **l.102 Crusoe's Isle:** the uninhabited island off the South American coast where Robinson Crusoe is shipwrecked in Daniel Defoe's novel (1719). **l.113 Sir Walter:** Sir Walter Scott (1771–1832), Scottish novelist and poet. **l.115 That Fairy-Helper:** probably a reference to the 'demon' Scott playfully claimed helped him to write his novels. **l.121 Arabian Nights:** first popularized in Europe in Antoine Galland's French translation (1704–7); anonymously translated into English in 1706–21. **l.123 Quarles' Emblems:** poems by Francis Quarles (1592–1644), with engravings, first published in 1635; **Esop's Fables:** moral stories by or attributed to the quasi-historical Æsop (*fl.* 6th century BC). **l.126 Doctor Coote:** Charles Coote (1761–1835), historian. **l.132 Tyburn's palmy days:** Tyburn was London's place of public execution until 1783. **l.333 Narcissus:** in Greek myth, a beautiful youth who fell in love with his own reflection. **l.395 *Joseph*:** see Genesis 39. **l.422 Banditti:** term for picturesque Italian outlaws. **l.428 Titian:** Tiziano Vecelli (*c.* 1477–1576), Venetian painter; **Guido:** Guido Reni (1575–1642), Italian painter. **l.429 Claude:** Claude Lorrain (1600–82), French landscape painter. **l.439 Gerard Dow:** Gerard Dou or Dow (1613–75), Dutch painter. **l.453 Sir Joshua:** Sir Joshua Reynolds (1723–92), English painter. **ll.463–72 A holy pilgrim . . . as we behold:** this is based on 'The Story of Zobeide' in the *Arabian Nights*. **l.558 Bishop Hatto:** according to legend, Hatto, Archbishop of Mainz, was eaten alive by mice or rats in a tower to which he had fled in an attempt to escape them. **ll.612–15 But a bold prince . . . airy course:** Crabbe is recalling, not wholly accurately, Prince Agib's story in 'The History of the Third Calender, a King's Son', in the *Arabian Nights*. **l.669 Caliph Haroun:** Haroun-al-Raschid (763–809), Caliph of Baghdad, a central figure in many of the tales of the *Arabian Nights*. **l.670 David and Goliath:** see 1 Samuel 17. **ll.680–1 The mountain loadstone . . . ships on shore:** see 'The History of the Third Calender'.